# DON HAWKINS

# MASTER DISCIPLESHIP

*Jesus' Prayer and Plan for Every Believer*

kregel
RESOURCES

Grand Rapids, MI 49501

Cover photograph: Copyright © 1995, Kregel, Inc.
Cover and book design: Alan G. Hartman

**Library of Congress Cataloging-in-Publication Data**
Hawkins, Don.
    Master discipleship / Don Hawkins.
       p.  cm.
    Includes bibliographical references.
    1. Discipling (Christianity).  2. Evangelistic work.
I. Title.
BV4520.H38     1995     253—dc20     95–31366
                                      CIP

ISBN 0-8254-2866-1  (paperback)

1  2  3  4  5  Printing / Year  00  99  98  97  96

*Printed in the United States of America*

# CONTENTS

99801

# INTRODUCTION

I recognize that writing a book on discipleship isn't unique. Many gifted teachers and talented disciplers have written on the subject; however, I have yet to discover a book that zeros in on the one passage I consider to be the ultimate source of insight on the subject of discipling. *Master Discipleship* is designed to motivate us to fulfill Christ's final mandate to the church. Passed along from generation to generation, Christ's final mandate extends to all believers today.

The unique thesis of *Master Discipleship* is this: In His prayer to the Father recorded in John 17, the Lord Jesus gave His disciples *and* us an overview of all the essential ingredients of discipleship. From this passage we can follow, in His own words, the order and the methodology He used in the process of discipling others.

Thus *Master Discipleship* is designed to provide a twentieth-century perspective on what is essentially a first-century "how-to" discipleship manual. I'm convinced that pastors and others in full-time ministry, as well as concerned laypersons who wish to develop their skills in the discipling process, can benefit from this material. My goal is to challenge the body of Christ to take up the priority of discipling and to motivate my readers to become involved in the process.

# Acknowledgments

I want to express special appreciation to three men who did more than instruct me—they also discipled me: Alden Gannett, Phil Hook, and Charles Ryrie.

I also want to express my appreciation to three men who have given me the privilege of discipling them: Gary Purdy, Bill Campbell, and Scott Tibbels.

I'm grateful to be a part of this discipleship chain.

∞∞ ∞∞

I want to thank my wife, Kathy, for her persistent encouragement over many years that has brought this project from a series of messages to its present form.

My thanks also to Jim Kregel and Maury Lehmann of Kregel Publications for their vision for our ministry and to Kregel's Senior Editor, Dennis Hillman, and project editor, Helen Bell, for their attention to detail in the writing of this book; Dawn Leuschen for typing and retyping the manuscript, and Sandy Schindler, Allen Bean, and Brent Hawkins for important contributions.

# PART ONE

# DISCIPLING: WHAT IS IT?

The process of discipling is a lot like constructing a building. Jesus Himself pointed this out when He explained the cost of discipleship to the multitudes who followed Him (Luke 14:24–30). Whether you're constructing a brand new building, adding a new wing to an existing facility, or renovating an existing building for a new purpose, certain elements are essential in constructing either a building or a disciple.

First, you must begin with a plan. No successful building project was ever completed without the careful, detailed work of an architect or draftsman, and a successful discipleship program needs to be carefully planned.

Second, it's essential to count the cost. This was Jesus' main point when He told the story of someone reconstructing a tower without adequate financial provision. Many people today have suffered the shame and failure of cost overruns or insufficient funding through their failure to first count the cost. Discipleship costs everyone time, energy, and emotional involvement.

Third, the actual building must take place in an orderly process. It would be ludicrous to consider starting on the roof before finishing the foundation, and the same is true with building up the body of believers. As Paul pointed out in the context of building up the church, things must be done decently and in order (1 Cor. 14:40).

7

   *Master Discipleship* was written to describe this orderly
disciple-building process that the Lord has clearly laid out
for us to follow.

# Chapter One

# THE BIBLE'S
# DISCIPLING CHAPTER

In the early 1990s big business began focusing on a concept with roots in the first-century ministry of Jesus. It's a concept described today by the term *mentoring*, a technique designed to foster the growth of the next generation of leaders and managers. The latest buzzword used to describe mentoring, according to Massachusetts psychologist Harry Levenson, is generativity.[1] According to Dr. Levenson, generativity, or fostering the growth of the next generation, may provide the ultimate antidote to the greedy, grasping eighties. Dr. Levenson suggests that by mentoring subordinates and treasuring a company's long-term development, generative employees both energize the workplace and empower themselves.

Many people who have studied the church at the end of the twentieth century have suggested Christians could use a healthy dose of energizing and empowerment. To a great degree the church today has adopted the consumer mentality of Western culture. Many Christians attend church only when they feel like it, spend very little time studying the Bible, and show little interest in reaching a world in desperate need of the readily available Water of Life.

Addressing the National Religious Broadcasters recently, Bill Bright, founder of Campus Crusade for Christ, lamented the fact that far less than half of those who profess to be Christians regularly attend church. He stated that of the 100 million people in the United States who attend church on a fairly regular basis, 55 percent of them have indicated they are unsure of their own personal salvation. Only 2 percent regularly share their faith with others. Dr. Bright believes we need to do a better job of training disciples.

In one of his most recent annual surveys of lifestyles, values, and religious views, pollster George Barna noted that "on a given Sunday slightly less than half of all adults claim they attend worship services at a church. . . . What is most interesting about the decline in [church] attendance is that baby boomers, who had been exploring churches for the past five years, experienced a ten percentage point drop in attendance compared to one year earlier. Fifty percent of the boomers claim to have attended church services during the week preceding the survey in 1991; just 40 percent made the same claim in 1992. This decline cannot be explained away by sampling error."[2] Barna goes on to note that among self-described Christians one out of every five said they generally do not attend services. One-third of the group said they attend one to three times a month and only 40 percent claimed to attend services four or more times each month.

Now, church attendance is only one way to measure spiritual interest, commitment, or growth. The bottom line is, however, whether you're looking at church attendance, involvement in leading others to faith, commitment to serving the Lord, or evidencing the fruit of the Spirit, there's a notable lack of vitality and growth today in the lives of many who know the Savior. The question facing us is, How do we develop commitment, foster growth, and motivate God's people to Christlike service?

I believe the answer to that question parallels the concepts of mentoring and generativity that have come into vogue in modern business. They are relational techniques developed and refined to their highest forms by Jesus that we refer to today as "discipling."

## KEY DISCIPLESHIP SCRIPTURES

Discipleship has been a matter of significant interest in the Christian community. Numerous excellent books have been written on the subject. Detailed programs, complete with manuals and instructions, have been developed and implemented in local churches and among campus groups. *Master Discipleship* doesn't purport to take the place of any of these efforts. My goal is not to "rehash" what others have done on the subject of discipleship. My plan is to take a different tack entirely.

Some time ago I was visiting a respected pastor friend when the subject of discipleship came up. "Don," he told me, "if I had a dollar for every book on discipleship I've come across, I'd probably be able to buy a number of additional volumes for my library!" I agreed with him and then asked, "How many of those books deal in depth with the key passage of Scripture on discipleship?" He countered my inquiry with questions of his own, "What chapter do you have in mind? What passage do you consider to be the ultimate source of insight on the subject?" He then showed his knowledge of what Scripture has to say on the subject by suggesting two possible passages—Matthew 28:19 and 2 Timothy 2:2. I agreed with his assessment that those passages provide a great deal of insight on the subject of discipling, and we took the time to look together at both passages to see what they contributed to our understanding of the discipling process.

Typically we refer to Matthew 28:19–20 as The Great Commission. All four of the Gospels, plus the book of Acts, provide insight into the final commission the Lord gave His followers. Although most people who casually read Matthew 28:19 think the emphasis is on *going*, the major thrust of the passage is actually on *making* disciples who will then teach others. After reinforcing the authority He had been given, the foundation for His commission, Jesus instructed His followers to disciple all nations. The development of the passage suggests a threefold process for carrying out this mission: going, baptizing, and teaching.

*Going* clearly implies an effort on the part of Jesus' followers to make contact with those who will become the objects of discipleship. This mandate stands in stark contrast to the Old Testament emphasis on people of the Gentiles "coming" to the Lord God through Israel.

*Baptizing* underscores the importance of leading people to personal faith and having them give public testimony to that faith. Although in some circles baptism has been relegated to the position of an unimportant ritual or ordinance, the early church provided the line of demarcation for those who embraced the faith. Even today in many cultures across the world, an individual can verbally profess faith in Christ without a great deal of reaction from family or friends. However, as a missionary friend once told me, "Just let them be baptized, and their family rejects them, their pictures are turned to the wall, and they're treated like they never even existed."

*Teaching* is not simply the mastery of a set of facts or a system of doctrines; rather, Jesus urged His disciples to do as He had done with them—teach with the goal of fostering obedience. This was the kind of teaching Paul described in his own ministry as he stood on the shore at Miletus and told the elders from the church in Ephesus, "how I kept back nothing that was helpful, but proclaimed it to you, and taught you publicly and from house to house. . . . I have not shunned to declare to you the whole counsel of God" (Acts 20:20, 27).

We do not fulfill the Great Commission or the mandate in 2 Timothy 2:2 simply by sending missionaries or winning converts. The process of discipling includes reaching out to those who do not know the Savior, winning them to faith and allowing them to publicly declare that faith through baptism, then instructing them in the whole counsel of God. "As the Father has sent Me, I also send you" (John 20:21).

## FRAMEWORK FOR DISCIPLESHIP—JOHN 17

As my pastor friend and I discussed these passages together, I suggested to him that John 20:21 contained an important clue to figuring out the key chapter on discipleship in the New Testament. Since he believed strongly in the process of discipleship and had practiced it in his ministry, he was interested in finding out what passage I had in mind. He also didn't hesitate to reaffirm his own opinion that Matthew 28:19 and 2 Timothy 2:2 were the key passages on discipling in the New Testament.

Since we had only a short time left in our visit and were planning to get together the following week, I asked him to read carefully John 17, keeping in mind Jesus' phrase, "As the Father has sent Me, I also send you." I encouraged him

to look at John 17:4 and consider the phrase, "I have finished the work which You have given Me to do." I suggested
he read carefully through the chapter, looking for any statements that resembled "work" Jesus might have done on
behalf of the Father and noting both the nature and the objects of the work. After confirming the time we planned to
meet the following week, I left.

What I was sharing with my friend and urging him to discover was something I had discovered myself several years
before while preparing a series of messages on the Upper
Room Discourse. In a nutshell, my discovery was that John
17 not only contained what we might ultimately call the
Lord's Prayer, since it took the nature of a conversation between Jesus and His Father, which the disciples were privileged to hear, it also provided a framework for the process
of discipleship. This process was mandated by Jesus in His
final words in Matthew, implemented by Paul in his charge
to Timothy (2 Tim. 2:2), and is urgently needed if we are to
have a strong, vital church and an effective witness for Christ
today.

Two people, Mrs. Evelyn Jones and Dr. Howard Hendricks,
have helped me understand this key process.

Mrs. Jones taught high school English back in Alabama
when I was growing up, and she drilled into me and my
classmates the importance of nouns, verbs, objects, and
other parts of speech. In fact, I still have copies of the notes
I took giving the seven properties of a verb, the six properties of a noun, and details concerning the other parts of
speech.

Evelyn Jones didn't disciple me in the faith, but she taught
me some of the most important and useful lessons I've ever
learned, lessons that affect my study of the Word to this day!

Howard Hendricks did mentor me in the faith. One of
the first courses I took under him at Dallas Seminary was
called Bible Study Methods. In this class Professor
Hendricks urged us to "tear the bandages from our eyes"
and look at passages we may have studied many times as
if we had never seen them before. It was that process that
originally caused the insights on discipleship to almost
leap into my mind from the page in John 17. Several long
phrases from that chapter drove me to the conclusion that,
just as Hebrews 11 is the faith chapter in Scripture and

1 Corinthians 13 is the love chapter, John 17 is the discipling chapter, the passage that gives us the greatest insight on that strategic process.

This may be a good time to take a few moments, set aside this book, and read through John 17 in the way I suggested to my pastor friend. I would encourage you to read the chapter at least five times. Perhaps at least one of those times should include the entire Upper Room Discourse, beginning with the John 13. As you read through chapter 17, look for the "I" statements Jesus made. See what you discover!

## DISCIPLE AS STUDENT

Let's see if we can get the picture in focus. Jesus had invested three years in the lives of His followers. He had called them from a variety of activities—including fishing, tax collecting, and political activism—to follow Him. And follow Him they did, in the custom of young men of that day who would attach themselves to rabbis in order to learn from them.

In fact, the word *disciple* comes from the Greek word *manthanō*. The basic meaning of *disciple*, according to Webster, is a pupil, follower, or learner.[3] Greek language authorities Arndt and Gingrich define the term *manthanō* as "to learn, appropriate to oneself, best through instruction and through experience or practice."[4] Other authorities describe a disciple as a pupil or scholar (Matt. 10:24), especially the follower of a public teacher like John the Baptist.

Before the days of Socrates, this word described the process by which a disciple or *mathetés* attached himself to a teacher in order to gain either theoretical or practical knowledge. It was frequently used for the adherents of the philosophical schools of early Greece. Later its use was extended to the process of apprenticeship by which a young man learned a trade.[5]

In the Judaism of Jesus' day *manthanō* described the process by which a person mastered Judaic traditions by becoming the disciple of a recognized rabbi or master. Only through participating in this process could an individual become recognized as a teacher of the Law and win the right to teach others. Typically, as did Jesus' disciples, such students left home and lived with the teacher. They listened, learned, and observed, because "a disciple was expected to both learn all the rabbi knew and to become like him in piety and character."[6]

In similar fashion, Jesus took these selected men, invested time in their lives, and mentored or discipled them. His goal in this process can be seen in a statement He made to them in one of His early sermons, "A disciple is not above his teacher, but everyone who is perfectly trained will be like his teacher" (Luke 6:40).

Two important principles can be identified from Jesus' simple statement. First, discipling involves more than just dialogue. It implies a relationship of respect, learning, and submission—an attitude of "teachability" is essential. Furthermore, the ultimate goal of discipling is to change behavior, not simply communicate content. Ultimately, those who become full-grown or mature will be more like the discipler or teacher. The implications for discipling today are clear. When we disciple, our goal is to produce Christlikeness in those we mentor.

## GOD'S PROVISION

In this verse Jesus used a fascinating verb, one frequently found in Scripture, to describe the product of discipleship. The word is *katartizō*, a term which means to be completely furnished or equipped. It was a term that might be used in first-century society of a physician setting a broken bone. It was used to describe the process of outfitting a ship that was about to sail with the supplies and furnishings needed by those on board. Both Matthew and Mark employed the word to describe the process of mending or repairing torn fishing nets (Matt. 4:21, Mark 1:19). Later Paul would use it to explain the procedure for restoring one who had clearly stepped outside the bounds of Christian propriety (Gal. 6:1).

The various uses of this word have important implications in terms of discipleship. As disciples of Christ sail the sea of life, they need adequate spiritual food. When they step out of bounds, they will need to be restored to fellowship. When aspects of their lives have become torn and broken, they need to be mended, repaired, or healed. The ultimate goal must always be to bring them along to maximum maturity and Christlikeness.

## How the Process Works

How do we accomplish this process? How should we disciple? Many of the books that have been written on the subject have addressed themselves to putting together a framework based on various statements in the New Testament. While these studies can be extremely valuable, what I have learned from digging into John 17 leads me to conclude that this passage provides the fountainhead and the ultimate framework for the process of discipling. In a sense, you might say going back to John 17 is like visiting the headwaters of the Mississippi River in Minnesota. Though the appearance of the river may be somewhat different from that of the waters that flow past the arch in St. Louis, the bridge in Cairo, Illinois, or the levees of New Orleans, the river is never more pure or less polluted than it is at its headwaters.

So let's step back again for some background to that Passover meal in the Upper Room where twelve men reclined around a table and listened to the final extended discourse of the Man who for three years had mentored them, pointing them by word and example to His Father.

One of those men, the apostle John, prefaced his record of the evening by underscoring two important concerns in the mind of Jesus. One was the certain knowledge that He was about to leave His men; the other was His deep commitment and love for them.

Fully aware of the authority and mission He had received from the Father, Jesus laid aside the robe designating Him as a rabbi, took a towel, and fulfilled the role of a servant by washing the disciples' feet. The disciples couldn't miss their Master's point. He had provided for them the example—a pattern so they might conduct themselves as He had (13:15–16).

The disciples must have felt a bit of sensory overload as event followed event that evening. First, Jesus indicated that one of the disciples would betray Him. Then Judas, after receiving the sop—a piece of bread dipped in the bowl of Passover spices, a symbol of great honor—left the meeting. When he was gone, Jesus told the remaining disciples, "Now the Son of Man is glorified, and God is glorified in Him" (v. 31). In view of the coming separation, He was leaving them with a major mandate—to love each other as He, Christ, had loved them—a mandate that would become the badge of their discipleship (vv. 34–35).

When Jesus said, "By this all will know that you are My disciples," the emphatic word placed at the beginning of the sentence is *My*. In other words, the important element is that people be able to see that the disciples are His followers. So it is with us and those we disciple today. Our goal is not to produce followers of ourselves or of any other human leader. Our objective is to make disciples of Christ.

The disciples, however, were having trouble concentrating on Jesus' mandate to love. Simon Peter voiced their main concern, "Lord, where are You going?" (v. 36). Their hearts were agitated, but Jesus gave them encouragement, letting them know that His plan included returning to take them into His presence (14:3), underscoring the importance of their enduring faith in Him (vv. 10–12), promising them the resource of answered prayer plus the ultimate power of the indwelling Spirit (vv. 13–14, 16–17, 25), and then providing them with His peace (v. 27).

Realizing their need to understand and apply the truth of His power, He used the analogy of a vine and branches to challenge them to fruitfulness and loving service (15:1–16). He warned them of the hostility of a world system that hated Him (vv. 18–19), urging them to be prepared for persecution (vv. 20–21), and reminding them that, empowered by the Holy Spirit, they would tell the world about Him since they had been with Him (vv. 26–27).

As they continued to listen, their minds became filled with consternation, confusion, and sorrow (16:6). Jesus reinforced the necessity for His departure from them to return to His Father. Then He elaborated on the empowering work of the Spirit of Truth in convincing people of their need of a Savior (vv. 8–11) and in directing His followers into all the truth (vv. 13–15).

When Jesus paused in His discourse, the disciples expressed their confusion to each other over His announcement that He would depart from them and then return (v. 17). Understanding their confusion, Jesus explained that their sorrow and grief, although real, would ultimately turn into joy (v. 20). During His absence, they would have the right, based on Jesus' name and authority, to pray and receive God's provision (vv. 23–24). Furthermore, Jesus Himself promised to intercede for them, based on the Father's love for them (vv. 26–27).

In response, the disciples expressed the assurance of their faith in the Savior. Jesus then concluded His discussion with a reminder of impending tribulation set against His promise of peace and victory (vv. 32–33).

## His Mission and Theirs

If you and I had been in that group, we would undoubtedly have felt that same keen sense of grief and loss. We likely would not have understood the implications of Jesus' departure. Yet we couldn't help picking up on His message that we too had a mission, just as He had a mission in the world.

That brings us to the seventeenth chapter, where John and the other disciples were given the unique privilege to listen in on a conversation between God the Son and God the Father. Picture the Savior, surrounded by anxious disciples to whom He has just given His blessing of peace and His promise of victory in the face of tribulation, as He lifts His eyes to heaven.

He began by acknowledging "Father, the hour has come." Clearly, Jesus has the impending crucifixion in mind. No serious student of Scripture can miss this. The Son would glorify the Father by giving eternal life to those who come to know Him.

Then Jesus makes an amazing statement, "I have glorified You on the earth. I have finished the work which You have given Me to do" (v. 4).

What is Jesus saying here? That's the question that jumped into my mind as I attempted to read this passage as though I was seeing it for the very first time. What did He mean by "the work which You have given Me to do"?

Most people tend to relate this work to the Cross and His earlier statement, "The hour has come." Yet there seems to be a clear contrast in tense between the past "I have finished the work You gave Me to do," and the work He is about to undertake, referred to in the phrase "The hour is come." I felt this was reinforced as I read through John 17, noting the statements Jesus made to the Father in which He described the work He had accomplished with His disciples. It almost seems redundant to label this work discipleship, but that's exactly what it was.

## SIX STEPS TO CHRISTLIKE DISCIPLESHIP

It is this outline that I hoped my pastor friend would discover as he examined John 17. I believe Jesus, in talking with His Father, knowing His disciples were listening in, purposefully outlined the steps He had taken—and their logical sequence—to show them and us exactly how this process of discipleship works.

- I have manifested Your name to the men You have given Me out of the world (v. 6).
- For I have given to them the words which You have given Me (v. 8).
- I pray for them (v. 9).
- I kept them in Your name (v. 12).
- I have given them Your Word (v 14).
- I also have sent them into the world (v. 18).

My purpose in this book is to develop these six steps that Jesus Himself took with His disciples and see how they apply to discipling today.

| | | |
|---|---|---|
| Discipleship Step 1 | *Example* | I have manifested Your name to the men (John 17:6). |
| Discipleship Step 2 | *Evangelism* | I have given them the words [the Gospel (John 17:8). |
| Discipleship Step 3 | *Intercession* | I pray for them (John 17:9). |
| Discipleship Step 4 | *Encouragement* | I kept them in Your name (John 17:12). |

| Discipleship Step 5 | *Edification* | I have given them Your Word (John 17:14). |
|---|---|---|
| Discipleship Step 6 | *Extension* | I also have sent them into the world (John 17:18). |

When I met with my pastor friend the following week, I observed a twinkle in his eyes as he opened his Bible and showed me the notes he had written down. He had identified all six of the statements Jesus had made, and his reaction was similar to mine when I first made this discovery. "I can't believe I never saw this before, Don! It's right there in the text!" I explained to him that I'd had the same reaction. I'd studied the passage on several occasions, taught it, preached from it, yet had never seen the obvious outline of the process of discipleship.

"What set it off for me was that phrase *I have finished the work*," he said. I smiled and nodded, agreeing that this had been a key for me as well.

Then he asked, "Did it concern you that the word *disciple* or *discipleship* isn't even found in John 17?" I thought about that and we discussed it further. While the word *disciple* is found seven times in the Upper Room Discourse in chapters 13–16, I didn't feel that the presence or absence of the term in this passage was the "make or break" criteria. After all, I view 1 Corinthians 15 as the key chapter on hope in the New Testament, although the word hope appears only once in the entire chapter. Yet anyone who reads 1 Corinthians 15 can't miss the message of hope that it contains. My friend and I agreed that the same was true of John 17 as the most important chapter on discipleship.

### CALL TO COMMITMENT

The term *disciple* is most commonly used in the New Testament to designate the twelve men who were chosen by Jesus to be with Him and then sent forth to represent and serve Him (Mark 3:14). They had been trained in the same way the rabbis of Jesus' day trained those who followed and learned from them. The process involved a commitment to learn from and become like their master (Luke 6:38), and a commitment to persevere as disciples, making the process of discipleship the priority of life (14:26). As William McDonald so clearly pointed out in his publication *True Discipleship*:

> The Savior is not looking for men and women who will give their spare evenings to Him—or their weekends— or their years of retirement. Rather, He seeks those who will give Him first place in their lives.[7]

## Consuming Love for Christ

What kind of commitment does this kind of discipleship take? First of all, it calls for a consuming love for Jesus. In Luke 14 Jesus began His final journey toward Jerusalem where He would give His life for the sins of the world. His disciples were with Him and a great multitude followed along. Turning to the crowd, He said, "If anyone comes to Me and does not hate his father and mother, wife and children, brothers and sisters, yes, and his own life also, he cannot be My disciple" (v. 26).

What exactly did Jesus mean by these enigmatic words? Was He advocating hostility toward parents, abusive anger, or caustic indifference toward spouse, children, or family? Could He have even meant that we are to become self-abusive or engage in some kind of bizarre, masochistic behavior?

Using a common teaching method of His day, it seems Jesus was placing the emphasis on the intensity of relationship, the degree of commitment. What He was saying is consistent with His message elsewhere in the Gospels. A true disciple is one who loves Jesus more than anyone or anything else. His point was not to encourage animosity or even rejection of other relationships that are given priority elsewhere in Scripture. Rather, the grateful love for Jesus that fills our hearts in response to His sacrificial death for us should be so great that every other relationship would pale in comparison—even to the point of looking like hatred.

Our loving relationship with the Son of God must reign supreme, overshadowing all human relationships. Clearly we are to demonstrate love in our human relationships, for Jesus encouraged His disciples in John 13:34–35 to do just that. The Lord's emphasis in Luke 14:26 was one of degree, and the ultimate degree of love is to be seen in our relationship with Christ.

### Identifying with Christ

Second, such a commitment involves a choice to identify with Jesus. In the following statement (14:27), Jesus pointed out that whoever does not bear His cross cannot be His disciple. In an era characterized by metallic crosses and other religious trinkets worn as jewelry, there may be some confusion about what Jesus meant by the term *bear His cross*. Now, I'm not condemning people who chose to wear gold or silver crosses, but that's not what Jesus had in mind here. Nor do I think He's talking about some kind of physical suffering, personal relationship, or emotional pain. I've had numerous people say to me, "My alcoholic husband is the cross I bear" or "I've had cancer for years—that's my cross."

I'm convinced that we must view the terminology of the cross through the lens of the first century. The cross was what a criminal who had been condemned to die carried from the place where he was sentenced to the place where he was put to death. Thus it became a form of identification, a symbol of shame and dishonor.

In today's world we love to heap honors on people, usually those who occupy roles we covet ourselves. The world passes out its Oscars, Emmys, Golden Globes, Heismans, MVPs, Pulitzers, and Nobel Prizes. Even in the Christian community we recognize books and ministries with coveted awards.

While nothing in Scripture condemns legitimate recognition, the major emphasis Jesus gives His disciples was on humility and a willingness to suffer dishonor and reproach. Over and over He told them, "The servant is not greater than his master." "If they persecute Me, they will persecute you." It seems bearing this cross involves a willingness to identify with Jesus Christ—even when it may bring suffering and shame.

It is interesting that Jesus' following words encouraged His followers to count the cost. Using the illustration of building a tower or waging war, Jesus urged them to make sure they count the cost, even to the extent that they forsake all that they have in order to be His disciple (14:33).

## Following Christ

Third, this commitment required following Jesus. In addition to a surpassing love and self-denial, Jesus pointed out to His followers that those who are His disciples would keep following Him. It wasn't simply that their paths would cross on occasion or that they might spend some time together. The custom of Jesus' day dictated that men who wanted to become disciples of certain rabbis made following the teacher a higher priority than their occupation or any other pursuit. Following a person this way involves a number of important concepts—imitation, passion, obedience—and these become the forces that govern the life of the one who follows Christ.

You can't be around my friend James very long before you realize his passion for military service. James is a career marine. Clearly the slogan "The Marines are looking for a few good men" fits James perfectly. Tall and muscular, with steel-gray eyes, sharp cheekbones, and close-cropped, sandy-blond hair, James carries himself with military bearing. He eats, sleeps, and lives the corps.

Because he is in the military, James gives unquestioning obedience to his superior officers. He wouldn't dream of arguing, even when he may have questions in his mind about orders he has been given. Since the time he entered boot camp many years ago, his goal has been to become like the drill instructors who taught him the basics of military service. And he has become proficient in following their example.

### PLACING PRIORITY ON DISCIPLESHIP

So how does this process of discipleship relate to our priority mandates? Throughout the Gospels Jesus established two priority mandates:

- loving God wholeheartedly
- loving people unconditionally

We will discuss these and how they relate to the process of discipleship in further detail in chapter 2 after we first consider the question, "What is a disciple?" However, without question the process of discipling can move both those who *are* discipled and those *who* disciple toward a more intense, passionate love for the Lord and a greater love for people. When it fulfills these objectives, discipleship is working as it should.

## ENDNOTES

1. *Psychology Today* 25 (November/December 1992): 10.
2. George Barna, *The Barna Report* (Ventura, Calif.: Regal Books, 1992–93), 92.
3. *Webster's New World Dictionary of the English Language* (N.Y.: World, 1963), 136.
4. William F. Arndt and F. Wilbur Gingrich, *A Greek-English Lexicon of the New Testament, and Other Early Christian Literature* (Chicago: University of Chicago, 1957), 491.
5. For an excellent discussion of the history of this word see Lawrence O. Richards, "The Disappearing Disciple: Why Is the Use of Disciple Limited to the Gospels and Acts?" *Evangelical Journal* 11 (1992): 3ff.
6. Ibid., 5.
7. William McDonald, *True Discipleship* (Kansas City, Kans.: Walterick Publishers, 1975), 5.

# Chapter Two

---

# WHAT IS A DISCIPLE?

I felt my excitement rising as I locked my car and walked from the parking lot toward the entrance of a north Dallas hotel. A hot brisk wind from the southwest ruffled my hair. I hardly noticed because I was excited about meeting with Bill, Scott, and Gary, the men who had asked me to disciple them. We had been meeting regularly for lunch and Bible study at the hotel coffee shop, just a few blocks from where we all worked. I'd had the privilege of discipling others during my years in the pastorate and in Christian radio, but I had never had a group of men come to me and ask that I disciple them. Well, *ask* wasn't really the right word. They actually insisted, and I've been glad they did.

On this particular occasion, after making our way through the salad bar, finishing our lunch, and securing refills of lemonade and ice tea, the four of us moved from discussing what was happening in our lives to the topic at hand—what is a disciple?

Gary, who has taught Sunday school for a number of years, went first. "There's a way I've heard the word used," he began, "but I'm not sure it's accurate. Some time ago I heard a speaker challenge Christians to step it up a notch from their ordinary lives and become real disciples. Maybe it's a little bit like flying. You know, most Christians fly coach, but disciples go first class."

Bill leaned forward in his seat and chimed in, "You mean all Christians are like members of the Dallas Cowboys football team, and disciples are the starters?"

Scott, tall and athletic and a motivational speaker, continued the conversation, "Interesting you should bring that up. I've heard the word used the same way and, frankly, I don't buy it."

"Why not?" I asked, remembering an article I had read in the library at Dallas Seminary the day before. "What bothers you about that concept?"

"For one thing," Scott replied, "the word means a learner or a student, doesn't it? Seems to me like a student is a student—not someone of superior rank."

"What about all those calls to commitment that are associated with discipleship?" Bill interjected. "Just a couple of weeks ago at church our pastor was making the point that discipleship wasn't the same as run-of-the-mill Christianity."

Turning to me, Bill's gray eyes sparkled. He smiled and said, "Come on, Hawkins, take a position on this issue!"

## DISCIPLE OR CHRISTIAN?

"Great discussion, guys," I began. "You've isolated what I think is one of the most important concerns to address when we wrestle with the question of discipleship. I do agree that the call to discipleship we find coming from Jesus in the New Testament is a call to something above and beyond the ordinary. But I don't think the term was ever designed to differentiate disciples from less-committed Christians. In fact, I want to stretch your thinking today. I believe it's possible for a man to become a disciple before he ever becomes a Christian."

Immediately my three companions began shaking their heads with varying degrees of vigor. "I don't think so," replied Bill, the first to voice his disagreement.

"Hold that thought for a second," I replied. "Let me share something with you I discovered yesterday. Here's a quote from Joe Aldrich from an article in *Discipleship Journal*. The article has a great title, 'How Do You Turn a Frog Into a Prince?' Now, Joe has studied the Word for quite a few years. Here's what he says, 'Of the 270 occurrences of "disciple" in the Gospels and Acts, the word is never used to set apart more devout believers from run-of-the-mill believers—a common way we use it today.'"[1]

Looking up from my quote, I noticed all three of my companions' heads were again nodding agreement. "Another thing Aldrich points out in this article is that the use of the word stops at the end of Acts. In fact, the last New Testament use of the word *disciple* is Acts 21:16, in the Epistles it's *believers, brothers,* and *saints.*"

Gary, the oldest of our group, jumped in. "So, do you think it means discipleship was only for the first century? I came across an article entitled 'The Disappearing Disciple' that pointed out the same thing. The author seemed to suggest that maybe discipling was for Jesus in His day, but that shepherding and body life had sort of taken the place of discipleship today."[2]

"I'm familiar with the article you're talking about, Gary. I respect the author and agree with a lot of his conclusions. One of his major concerns is that people who disciple today tend to set themselves up as authorities over people they disciple. They make disciples of themselves rather than of Christ. I think that's a legitimate concern, but I don't agree that the absence of the word for discipling in the Epistles means the process ended, or that once the disciples started being called Christians, they didn't disciple anymore."

## DISCIPLES AND ANTIOCH

We began looking at Acts 11, where a large number of people in Antioch, the third largest city in the world, had become believers. As the four of us pored over two paragraphs in Acts 11:19–26, we noticed several parallel processes in operation at the same time.

Believers who had been forced to leave Jerusalem because of persecution for preaching the Word and the Lord Jesus (vv. 19–20). According to Luke's record a great number believed and turned to the Lord in response to their preaching (v. 21). Clearly evangelism was taking place. The followers of Jesus had gone to Antioch, proclaimed the Lord Jesus, and seen individuals in large numbers identify with the Savior. Although baptism isn't specifically mentioned here, it is highly likely, based on the rest of the book of Acts, that these converts participated in water baptism to publicly declare their new faith.

However, the church leaders in Jerusalem recognized the need for more than just winning converts. The man they selected from their company to carry out the next phase of "Operation Antioch" was Barnabas, unquestionably the most gifted encourager in the early church.

As the four of us continued our examination of the passage, I asked them to identify the specific things that Barnabas did in Antioch. They came up with a fabulous list—first he looked to see what God had been doing, he responded enthusiastically to what he saw, he began encouraging them all to strengthen their commitment to the Lord, he lived the life before them, he continued leading people to the Savior, he sought additional help from Saul, he kept meeting with the believers for an extended time, he taught them many things.

Finally, we came to the climactic statement summarizing the ministry of Barnabas, "And the disciples were called Christians first in Antioch." "So what does that mean?" I asked.

Gary immediately responded, "I don't think it means they stopped being disciples and started being Christians, or that discipleship ended here. It seems to me this is the Lord's way of moving the emphasis from the process of discipleship to its purpose—to help people develop as followers of Christ."

"Absolutely," Scott continued. "After all, if you look back at the Great Commission in Matthew 28:19, you see everything Jesus told them to do there happening here in Antioch."

"Exactly," Bill continued. "They went to Antioch, evangelized people there, then Barnabas and Saul taught them how to live as disciples. So they were called Christians because they became Christlike."

Sitting back in my chair to take a sip of lemonade, I smiled broadly. "You guys are great," I said. "You just nailed down in less than ten minutes what I figured would take us an hour to cover—and you sure didn't need me to lay it out for you!"

## THE ESSENCE OF DISCIPLESHIP

What I had been seeing in the lives of Scott, Bill, and Gary is the essence of what our subject is about. Discipleship involves life-changing learning in the context of relationships that leads to Christlikeness.

### Learning

You cannot be a disciple unless you learn. Unfortunately, just being exposed to the truth doesn't necessarily involve learning the truth. I recall a statement one of my professors at Dallas Seminary made about one of my former classmates. Rolling his eyes a bit, the professor said, "He was enrolled in my class, but he was never one of my students." Unfortunately today there are individuals who enroll in discipleship programs who fail to learn and who do not grow. Surrounded by the truth, they never even seem to stumble into it, much less learn how to use it. In other words, when there is no learning, there is no discipling.

Early in His ministry, Jesus called Matthew (Levi as he had been known) to become one of His disciples. The Master was eating in Levi's home. The Pharisees, the religious leaders of the day, raised a question about the custom of fasting. In the process three groups of "disciples" were identified. Two, the disciples of John and of the Pharisees, practiced fasting, while Jesus' disciples did not. My point is that each of these groups of disciples learned a great deal when they became part of the discipleship process.

### Relationship

But even for those who followed the Pharisees and John, discipling involved more than simply attending classes or learning a set of facts. It involved a relationship. In one sense, those who followed John or the Pharisees had become participants in a particular movement. However, this was different from individuals today who decide to become a part of Greenpeace, the Republican National Committee, or the Rush Limbaugh "Dittoheads" fan club. While disciples may have become involved in a cause, their primary purpose was to learn, and learn they did—in relationship. We'll explore more of this later when we look at the call of the Twelve in Mark 3.

## Life-Changing

No one who looks at the record of the New Testament with an unbiased eye can deny the incredible transformation that took place in Peter and the other men who followed Jesus. They started out as professional fishermen, tax collectors, and political activists. One of their primary concerns throughout their time with Jesus was to argue the question of who would be first in the kingdom Jesus was going to establish. Frequently they displayed character weaknesses, emotional instability, spiritual ignorance, and blindness—at their better times!

Yet look at the picture Luke paints of these men following the resurrection and ascension of Jesus. We see them waiting in complete union and prayer for the fulfillment of the promise of the Holy Spirit (Acts 1:14). There's no debate here over what the Lord meant or worry about who will be greatest.

Then, on the Day of Pentecost each one became involved in communicating to the massive crowds in Jerusalem in the languages spoken by those individuals (2:6–8).

When their character was questioned by those who asserted that they must be drunk (v. 13), Peter responded boldly and compassionately, preaching the message that what the crowd had witnessed was in fulfillment of Joel's prophecy and that this was the time for those present to turn in faith and be baptized in testimony of their trust in Jesus as Messiah (v. 38). These men were already fulfilling Jesus' commission—going to the crowds in Jerusalem, sharing the Good News, baptizing believers. Then in the following days, they continued teaching the three thousand-plus who trusted the Savior at Pentecost (v. 42). Later they seized another opportunity to present the Gospel, and though they were arrested (4:3), five thousand new believers were added the next day! Hauled into court, Peter delivered a Spirit-filled message in which he declared that salvation was only through the name of Jesus Christ (v. 12).

Surprised by their boldness and recognizing that these men had no rabbinical training in their system, the leaders of Israel were forced to acknowledge that the disciples had been with Jesus (v. 13). Here were men whose lives had been transformed as they had learned in a relationship. Furthermore, their transformation had led to Christlikeness. The leaders were not impressed by any Pharisaic-style knowledge or an ability to debate the Scriptures. Rather they recognized that these men bore the marks of having spent time with the Man who claimed to be Israel's Messiah, who healed the sick, cast out demons, and raised the dead.

A few moments later in response to a command not to speak or teach in the name of Jesus, Peter and John responded with bold clarity: "Whether it is right in the sight of God to listen to you more than to God, you judge. For we cannot but speak the things which we have seen and heard" (vv. 19–20). Later, gathering with the other followers of Jesus, they prayed that God would sustain their boldness (v. 29)—and He did.

As more believers were added to the Lord (5:14), they were again arrested by the temple guards—and miraculously released by an angel from the Lord (5:17–19). Confronted once more by the religious leaders the following day in the temple, where they had returned to preach their message, and reminded of the strict edict not to teach in Jesus' name, they were accused of filling Jerusalem with their doctrine (v. 28). The charge was absolutely true, as Peter and the other apostles again reminded the Sanhedrin, the highest religious authority in Israel, that they were under moral and spiritual obligation to obey a higher authority—God Himself (v. 29).

Later, after being beaten and again ordered not to speak in the name of Jesus (v. 40), the men left the presence of the council "rejoicing that they were counted worthy to suffer shame for His name. And daily in the temple, and in every house, they did not cease teaching and preaching Jesus as the Christ" (vv. 41–42).

So what produced the dramatic difference in the lives of these men? To understand what took place, it may help us to revisit an event that happened earlier in the ministry of Jesus. The Lord had spent approximately one year observing the individuals who followed Him. It had been a year of incredible popularity as throngs had flocked to His side to hear His message and witness His miraculous deeds. But already the religious leaders were watching for an opportunity to destroy Jesus (Mark 2:6; 3:6).

So Jesus withdrew with His disciples, and the great multitude followed Him; in fact, some people came from over fifty miles away. After a time of public ministry, Jesus went up into a mountain where He invited the specific individuals He wanted to follow Him. As we indicated before, these individuals had come to Him in a variety of ways. Now, however, He chose them specifically to function as disciples, appointed for a specific purpose. According to Luke 6:12, Jesus had spent the entire previous night in prayer. Without question this night was a watershed in the life of the Master. Furthermore, although Mark has used the word *disciple* in a more generic sense up to this point, from here on it seems only the Twelve are referred to by Mark as disciples.

In the twofold purpose for which Jesus appointed these men we see something of God's ultimate purposes for us in life as well as a reflection of the natural rhythm of life which is demonstrated throughout God's creation.

## DISCIPLES ARE CALLED TO BE WITH HIM

First, these men were called "to Himself" (6:14). They were to live with Him, talk with Him, travel with Him, observe Him, and learn from Him. The process was to develop a relationship of love and commitment.

Without question one of the most effective ways to learn from someone is to spend lots of time with him or her. That's also one of the ways you become more like another person. Furthermore, spending time with someone is one of the greatest evidences that you truly care about that person.

As I write these words, I'm sitting at a table in a rather cluttered study in our home in Lincoln, Nebraska. My notes are scattered on one side of a long table. Across the room my wife, Kathy, has been sitting for the past several hours, working on her own project, a book titled *The Heart of a Stranger*. For both of us, one of the greatest delights in life is to spend time together while we are writing. We may pause occasionally to bounce an idea off the other or offer a comment. Often we work for long stretches in a comfortable silence.

We've been married almost thirty years now, and while

we don't always get along perfectly, we're a lot closer than we were during our first years of marriage. We think alike much more often, we understand each other better, and we're each other's best friend and biggest fan. That's what spending time together can do.

And that's how it happened with these men. The more time they spent with Jesus, the more they understood His deep, abiding, unconditional love for them. And the more they responded to Him in love.

## DISCIPLES ARE SENT WITH HIS LOVE

The disciples weren't just called to spend time with Him. They were also sent forth with an important mission to fulfill. Obviously it would have been much more comfortable for them to simply spend the rest of their natural lives in physical proximity with the Savior. However, the Lord had another plan—they would be sent out on a multifaceted ministry that included both preaching and meeting physical, emotional, and spiritual needs. Their message was to proclaim the good news of the Savior they had come to know. They were to reinforce this message by becoming personally involved in the lives of people, demonstrating compassion, meeting physical and spiritual needs. To make this possible, the Lord invested them with the authority to heal sickness and cast out demons.

Why did Jesus choose these two specific purposes for the men He called? We might wonder why He chose them at this point in the second year of His earthly ministry, which was almost at the midpoint of His time on earth and during a time when growing popularity was being replaced by rising opposition.

I'm convinced one of the most important clues as to what the Lord had in mind can be discovered in an event Mark recorded during the final week of Jesus' life, during an extended controversy with the Herodians, the Sadducees, and the Pharisees. It seems one of the scribes—identified by Matthew as a Pharisee—who was listening to the dialogue between Jesus and the other religious leaders raised a question about what command was first in importance. Without hesitation Jesus responded:

"The first of all the commandments is, 'Hear, O Israel, the Lord our God, the Lord is one. And you shall love the Lord your God with all your heart, with all your soul, with all your mind, and with all your strength.' This is the first commandment. And the second, like it, is this: 'You shall love your neighbor as yourself.' There is no other commandment greater than these" (Mark 12:29–31).

Jesus had spoken to this issue earlier in His ministry when He told the story of the Good Samaritan (Luke 10:25–37). I am convinced that these mandates, while addressing often-considered questions from those who listened to Jesus in His day, also carry great significance for us today.

I think we can best see this significance when we distill these commandments from the Old Testament books of Deuteronomy and Leviticus into two summary statements.

- The initial command is to love the Lord God whole-heartedly.
- The second is to love people unconditionally.

In other words, wholehearted love for God and unconditional love for people are the ultimate mandates for those who follow God. Is it any wonder, then, that the Lord would select twelve disciples out of the core group of seventy-plus who followed Him, instruct them first to be with Him, then send them forth to minister to people? To spend time with Him was to cultivate that wholehearted love He considered the ultimate priority. Then they would be prepared to be sent forth to demonstrate that unconditional love for people He wanted them to model for a lost and hurting world.

There's an important lesson to learn in this event for those of us who would be His disciples today. If we want to be His disciples ourselves or if we wish to motivate others to become His disciples, we must seek a wholehearted love for God and an unconditional love for people—a heart for God that demonstrates itself in spending life-changing time with Him plus a wholehearted love for people that reaches out with God's life-giving message and with personal involvement in meeting the needs of those around us.

I am convinced that the more we grow as disciples, the greater will be our wholehearted love for God and our unconditional love for people. Furthermore, these two qualities will be at the top of the list of truths we seek to communicate by word and example to those we would disciple.

## THE NATURE OF A DISCIPLE

If spending time with Him and then being sent forth to represent Him to people describes the process that caused the disciples to become known as those who turned the world upside down for Christ, what has this taught us in terms of discipleship?

First, a disciple is one who has a relationship with his teacher. As we have noted, the beginning point for effective discipling, especially as it relates to the Twelve, was not simply knowledge, but knowledge in the context of relationship. Jesus didn't simply hand Peter, Andrew, James, and John a syllabus, a course description, or a bibliography. He didn't schedule five lectures one week, three lectures and an exam the next, or instruct them to write a term paper on Discipleship 101. Instead He developed a relationship with them, cultivating it over time. Effective discipleship always begins with a relationship. As Juan Carlos Ortiz points out in *Disciple*, "So discipleship is not a communication of knowledge or information, it is a communication of life. Discipleship is more than getting to know what the teacher knows, it is getting to be what he is."[3]

Second, a disciple receives knowledge from his teacher. There is an important principle of balance here. As Bill Hull explains, the Greek word for disciple, *mathetés*, "implies an intellectual process that directly affects the lifestyle of a person."[4] It's important not to go to the one extreme and turn discipleship into just an academic discipline, nor to the other extreme and remove all content. It's almost impossible to catalog everything the disciples learned factually during their time with Jesus. Yet the most important aspect of that learning was its impact on their lives.

Third, a disciple comes to reflect his teacher's values. That's why at Antioch the disciples ultimately came to be called "Christians," that is, "those who follow or imitate Christ" (Acts 11:26). Years ago I recall hearing my mentor, Alden Gannett, emphasize the fact that Barnabas did not exhort the believers in Antioch "that with purpose of heart

they would cling to Barnabas" (11:23). He continually encouraged them to remain true to the Lord, not himself. I've
never forgotten Dr. Gannett's point, and I'm convinced that
one of the greatest distortions of the discipleship process
occurs when those we disciple become more like us than
like our Savior. Sure, they may pick up some of our traits,
that's to be expected. I can readily identify elements of the
lives and ministries of people who have mentored me in
my own ministry. But these men didn't seek to turn me into
carbon copies of themselves. Their goal was to motivate me
to become more like Christ, to love Him wholeheartedly,
and through Him to love people unconditionally.

### PERSPECTIVE, PASSION, PLAN

As I left the hotel that hot summer afternoon after spending an exciting hour with these men who were eager to know
Jesus Christ better and communicate with Him more effectively, three observations struck me.

The first was a renewed perspective on the process of discipleship. It's a process that works. It is effective. Even
though we are to follow this process because Jesus dictated
that we do it, it's encouraging to know that it's a process that
*works*. The first century shows us just how effectively the
process works. These men were dramatically changed. They
became some of the most ultimate difference-makers who
ever lived. When we think of twentieth-century people who
have made a difference—the negative contributions of
Hitler and Saddam Hussein or the positive impact of Billy
Graham, Albert Schweitzer, and Mother Teresa—we still
conclude that these first-century difference-makers were in
a class by themselves.

Second, I was struck by the importance of developing a
passion for the person of the Lord Jesus. With our busy
lifestyles so many things clamor for our time, compete for
our attention, and distract us from what matters most.

The real issue is: What are the passionate concerns of our
lives? What really matters most to us? As I thought about this,
I reflected back to my college days in Alabama when Kathy
was in school in Louisiana. We were miles apart, but we spent
time together on the phone and corresponded with each
other. In fact, when I received letters from her, reading and

rereading them—even studying them for every nuance of meaning and detail—became both a priority and a passion. In addition, I looked for opportunities to spend time with her, sometimes driving all night to cover the five-hundred-mile distance between us in my red Volkswagon Beetle, then turning around to again drive through the night to get back for classes on Monday morning.

So as a disciple in process, I need to gauge my passion and priorities. Is my relationship with Jesus Christ at the center of what motivates and excites me as a person? That's passion. Further, do my schedule and activities indicate a significant amount of time spent in learning and following His directions? That's priorities.

Finally, I reflected on the importance of a realistic plan for reaching out to other people. It's not enough just to spend time with the Lord or study His word. I'm convinced He wants me involved in the lives of others. One of the greatest examples of this is the Good Samaritan. When the religious professionals didn't have the time and didn't seem to care, the Good Samaritan stopped, cared, and became involved. How can those of us who have come to know the Lord do any less?

I'm convinced that's part of what Paul had in mind when he wrote to Timothy, "And the things that you have heard from me among many witnesses, commit these to faithful men who will be able to teach others also" (2 Tim. 2:2).

In the next chapter, we'll focus the spotlight on the disciples—and see how Paul implemented the process of discipling in the life of Timothy, who became his son in the faith.

### ENDNOTES

1. Joe E. Aldrich, "How Do You Turn a Frog into a Prince?" *Discipleship Journal* (March 1991): 41.
2. Richards, "The Disappearing Disciple," 2–11.
3. Juan Carlos Ortiz, *Disciple* (Carol Stream, Ill.: Creation House, 1975), 105.
4. Bill Hull, *Jesus Christ, Disciple Maker* (Old Tappan, N.J.: Revell, 1973), 10.

## Chapter Three

# DISCIPLING: A PERSONAL PROCESS

They gathered by the thousands at the beautiful Lied Center in Lincoln, Nebraska, and in scores of other locations from coast to coast. Some were dressed in business suits or blazers. Others wore more casual attire—jeans, sweaters, slacks.

The occasion was a video conference seminar by Stephen Covey, one of the most respected management gurus of the nineties. His subject was a discussion of the principles contained in his best-selling management books *The Seven Habits of Highly Effective People, Principle-Centered Leadership,* and *First Things First.* Speaking to a live audience in Dallas, Texas, Covey spent half a day telling war stories, expounding on management principles, and explaining strategies for shared vision, mentoring, excellence, and passion.

Following the seminar I heard comments like "Great content—maybe not as organized as his book but still effective" or "Life-changing principles—especially his story about putting the big rocks in the jar first. I really want to make the main thing the main thing in my work." But the comment that grabbed my attention came a few days after the Covey seminar, and it went something like this: "It was a great seminar, and I just wish I could have become like him. I need to spend about a year with someone like

Stephen Covey so some of what he's talking about will rub off on me."

The biblical concept of discipleship is designed to make what that frustrated seminar attendee wished could happen actually happen. It's a process that was practiced by the most effective communicator who ever lived. Although He lived in the first century A.D., He understood more about people, mission, and change than Stephen Covey or any other twentieth-century authority has ever imagined.

Today we hear a lot of talk about mentoring, a term which has become increasingly popular. I've heard a variety of opinions about the difference between mentoring and discipleship. For purposes of discussion, I prefer to examine the similarities rather than the differences. Both happen in the context of relationships and involve time, process, and maturity. Both include the communication of facts with a focus on practical application, and both operate much in the same fashion as apprenticeships did in earlier cultures.

The most notable difference is that mentoring is a broader concept than discipling. Full professors can mentor instructors, Oscar-winning film directors can mentor key grips or production assistants, and money managers can mentor financial consultants. On the other hand, biblical discipleship zeros in on the process by which a person motivates another to become a fully-developing follower of Jesus Christ. Thus its content is uniquely biblical, its focus Christ-centered, and its purpose Christlike maturity. Discipling is one form of mentoring; in my judgment it is the most important form of all.

During his remarks at that seminar, Stephen Covey spoke highly of the process of mentoring, suggesting it could play a key role in bringing about positive changes in business itself and in the lives of those who are involved. As we examine the process of discipling, properly understood and employed, we see how it will benefit the church in the same way. I believe this not simply because of the pragmatic benefits of discipleship; rather, I see examples that flow out of the life of Jesus Christ.

## TIME INVESTMENT

Discipling was how Jesus invested the majority of His time here on earth. From the age of twelve the Master began declaring publicly His commitment to "be about My Father's business" (Luke 2:49). Throughout His years on earth, this determination surfaced time and time again. When the disciples expressed concern about His missing a meal, He countered by pointing out "My food is to do the will of Him who sent Me, and to finish His work" (John 4:34). When confronted with opposition, He focused on the works the Father had given Him to finish (5:17, 36). Fulfilling "the works of Him who sent Me while it is day" describes His passion for the three years of His earthly ministry (9:4).

What were the primary ways in which Jesus invested His days? Clearly He spent a great deal of time ministering to large groups of people. Frequently He preached—the Sermon on the Mount, the Sermon by the Seaside, many sermons along the way. Often He took time to heal the sick, open the eyes of the blind, or cause the lame to walk.

The ultimate focus of His life, though, was on the cross. As He said in Luke 19:10, "The Son of Man has come to seek and to save that which is lost." Without question the crowning work of His life was His substitutionary death on the cross followed by His resurrection the third day. The crown jewel of God's plan of redemption, the work of Christ in paying for our sins, clearly constituted the single most important work ever achieved, since it provides the foundation for individual salvation with the ultimate reversal of all the effects of the Fall and the establishment of a new heaven and earth in which righteousness will dwell.

However, a careful examination of the four Gospels shows another extremely important activity in which Jesus invested a significant amount of time. Over and over the gospel writers show Him in the company of a group of twelve men He gathered to be with Him. They walked together, ate together, lived as a family. They saw Him in the best of circumstances and in the worst. They were His men, and He invested His time discipling them. I believe one reason Jesus invested His time in these individuals was to motivate us to make discipling a priority today.

"But, Don," you may object, "my gift isn't discipling; it's preaching or teaching, encouraging, serving, or leading."

My response, friend, is that discipling isn't found on any of the lists of spiritual gifts. It's a mandate for us all. Whatever your gift is, God wants you to use it to motivate men and women to become fully-developed followers of Jesus Christ. How important is discipling? To find out, take the time to work your way through Matthew, Mark, Luke, and John. Keep a careful record of the amount of time Jesus spent with the multitudes, the time He spent alone, and the time He invested in His men. I think you'll catch a glimpse of the priority He gave the discipleship process.

## FINAL WORDS

The second reason the priority of discipleship stands out to me is that it was the last thing He talked about before He ascended into heaven. People have long recognized the value of last words. I still remember my father, who served in the Pacific theater during World War II, talk about Douglas MacArthur and his final words as he left the Philippines: "I shall return."

Matthew's record of Jesus' final words describes a meeting with the eleven disciples at a designated place. Though they worshiped Him, some—probably including Thomas and others—still struggled with their doubts.

First Jesus reminded them who was in charge—"All authority has been given to Me in heaven and on earth" (Matt. 28:18). What He was about to instruct them to do was not an option at additional cost, nor was it a suggestion they could mull over or consider. It was a command to be obeyed, given by the One who had the authority of heaven and earth. He didn't simply say, "Guys, if you learn how to do it and feel like doing it and have the time, try to work some discipling into your mix." Nor did He say, "You know, I really think discipling would be a good way to get things done. Why don't you give it a try?"

No, like a Marine Corps drill instructor or the general of the army mobilizing his troops, He gave His imperative: *make disciples.*

There's another element that stands out about Matthew 28:18–19. I've often heard missionaries, pastors, and others refer to this passage as the "marching orders" for the church. Actually, military authorities distinguish between marching orders and standing orders—standing orders determine what we are to keep in sight at all times. Standing orders allow us to have a standard against which we measure

progress because they define our ultimate goals. After reinforcing His authority, Jesus ordered His followers to pursue
a certain kind of ministry—discipling. Ultimately, these are
the church's "marching orders," as we will see in further
detail in the next chapter. All the other activities described
in Matthew 28:19–20 fit under the umbrella of the standing
order to disciple.

Here in Lincoln there are many excellent restaurants that
serve corn-fed Nebraska beef. Others feature seafood, Chi-
nese, or Thai menus. But anyone who has ever lived in Lincoln or any of the nearby cities and towns in Nebraska
automatically associates one word with a restaurant named
Valentino's—pizza. Long before we moved to Lincoln, we
had heard of the legendary pizzas served up by Valentino's.
Many people are convinced that there is no better pizza on
earth than the pies baked in the old ovens at the original
Valentino's restaurant.

Now Valentino's serves up the usual kinds of pizza—
pepperoni and mushroom, hamburger and sausage. They
fix a variety of specialty pizzas with multiple ingredients.
They even serve dessert pizzas. But the major focus at
Valentino's is on pizza, and pizza is what they do best.

There's a great lesson here for the church. Our churches
need good preaching and teaching that disciples. We need
effective counseling, small group ministries, benevolent
programs to meet the needs of those who suffer severe ill-
nesses, lose jobs, experience other personal disasters—all
to foster the process of discipling. Radio and television ministries can also have an effective impact, to the extent that
they lead to discipleship.

I've sought to make discipling a priority in all the ministries in which I've been involved. I spent a number of years
as a pastor. In each of the churches I was privileged to shepherd, I had the opportunity of personally discipling a number of men as a key part of my ministry. I've had the privilege
of mentoring individuals in the faith during my involvement
in Christian radio as well. Then, about a year after I began
developing the material for this book, a group of three businessmen in Dallas invited me to lunch in the coffee shop of
a north Dallas hotel. There they informed me that they had
been praying for God to provide someone to disciple them,
and they were convinced I was that someone! They gently

persisted despite my initial pleas that I was too busy. Ironically, what ultimately persuaded me to say yes to them was the realization that I had begun working on this book and that working through this material in the real-life context of discipling was important. Our relationship has now spanned three years and included studying the Word, fellowship, accountability, and growth. I've gained as much from the process as they have. So what I'm writing about comes out of the context of hearing and heeding the Master's command to just do it!

## PROVISION FOR THE JOB

There's a final element in this scene with Jesus and the disciples. Perhaps some of them looked at each other, shrugged their shoulders, at least inwardly, and said, "How can we?" After all, if they struggled with doubts before He gave them the command, think how they must have wrestled with the mandate to disciple. "We're just not up to the job," they might have thought.

Anticipating their insecurities and misgivings, the Lord coupled His command with a significant promise, "Lo, I am with you always, even to the end of the age" (Matt. 28:20).

What an amazing promise! We're not left to disciple others by ourselves. The Lord Himself is with us, watching us every step of the way, available for counsel at the lift of a prayer—even quicker than the drop of a hat! He has empowered us through His indwelling Spirit, giving us the wisdom, energy, and resources needed to fulfill the task at hand. Sure, it's a big task, but it's a doable task because He's made all the provision we need.

Some time ago I was in Birmingham, Alabama for a happy occasion—my parents' fiftieth wedding anniversary. As my brother Paul and I were making preparations for the festive occasion, we drove through Irondale, home of the legendary Whistle-Stop Cafe—the one that serves up the world-famous fried green tomatoes. My Uncle Don, for whom I was named, used to take me there for lunch. Near the cafe stands a two-story commercial building. Pointing to the building, I reminded my brother of the summer my uncle hired me to paint the concrete block structure. I remembered the first time I looked up at that building in the hot,

June Alabama sun. Those two stories seemed like a dozen! But my uncle had thought of everything I'd need—ladder, brushes, rollers, paint, buckets—even scaffolding for the highest parts. "I know it's a big job," he told me, "but I have confidence that you can do it. If you have any trouble what-soever, I'll be down here in the garage, just a whistle away. Call me whenever you need me."

I'm pleased to say that I was able to finish the job—in large measure because my uncle, who, like my father, had served in the marines, had mandated that I get the job done. I also knew he had provided everything I needed for the task and had promised to be with me. These, my friend, are the same resources we have available for the job of discipling.

## A PERSONAL PROCESS: OLD TESTAMENT EXAMPLES

Throughout the Bible we see examples of the value and effectiveness of this "personal" process; in fact, the founda-tion for personal discipling was laid in the Old Testament. Moses mentored Joshua, conveying a portion of his honor and power to the younger man (Num. 27:15–20). When Moses passed off the scene, Joshua was prepared to assume the mantle of leadership under God's authority (Josh. 1:1–9).

Elijah is another example. After a particularly draining epi-sode in his life—a time when he abandoned both his mission and his servant, his source of support—Elijah was rejuvenated by God and given the commission to anoint Elisha, a young man who would occupy the older prophet's attention until the end of his earthly life (1 Kings 19:15–16). Significantly, when Elijah encountered Elisha and placed his mantle on him—a phrase we still use today, similar to "passing on the baton"—Elisha killed the oxen he had been plowing with which had provided his means of personal support, left his people, and went with the prophet to serve him (vv. 19–21).

Later in Israel's history a former shepherd named David began collecting a group of men who traveled with him when he was fleeing from King Saul (1 Sam. 21:4–5). Before long the group had grown to approximately four hundred men, many of whom were in debt, discontented, or in some kind of distress (v. 2). These men watched David voice his faith in God (v. 3), receive instruction from God's prophet

(v. 5), ask God for direction about fighting the Philistines (23:2, 4), experience incredible victory (v. 5), trust God for protection day after day (v. 14), and receive encouragement from his close friendship with Jonathan (v. 16). Many of these very men ultimately became "heads of the mighty men" who gave David strong support in his kingdom (1 Chron. 11:10). How were they changed from the discouraged, disillusioned, and the distressed to the heroes, the leaders of Israel? Undoubtedly the example, encouragement, and instruction they received by being with David played a major role. They had been mentored by a man after God's own heart.

## A PERSONAL PROCESS: NEW TESTAMENT EXAMPLES

Following the example set by Jesus, the Lord's followers utilized this same approach. In Acts 11 Peter was called on the carpet by the church authorities in Jerusalem because they heard he had been preaching the Gospel to Gentiles— even going so far as to eat with them. In response, the apostle gave a detailed review of his experiences in the city of Joppa. During his time of prayer, God had granted a vision that was repeated three times—a sheet lowered from heaven containing animals both clean and unclean, kosher and common. Each time a voice urged Peter to kill and eat. Each time Peter refused and then heard the message, "What God has cleansed you must not call common."

Immediately after the vision three men arrived at the home where Peter was staying in Caesarea, inviting him to come at once to that Gentile city. It's significant to note Peter's words in Acts 11:12. Not only does Peter point out that the Spirit urged him to go with them without making any distinction, he adds, "These six brethren accompanied me, and we entered the man's house." We are not told who these six Christian brothers were who accompanied Peter, but it seems as though the Holy Spirit has given us an important clue into the way the apostles functioned in the first-century church. It appears Peter was investing his time in the lives of a small group of men.

This same pattern can be seen in the ministry of Paul, who spent a large amount of his time traveling throughout the Roman Empire to preach the Gospel. When the apostle taught and ministered in Ephesus for an extended period, he spent time with Gaius and Aristarchus of Macedonia, who were identified as his "companions in travel" (Acts 19:29). When they were arrested, the apostle wanted to go to their defense. Luke records that "the disciples permitted him not." Later, when Paul said farewell to the disciples of Ephesus and traveled back through Macedonia and into Asia Minor, he was accompanied by Sopater of Berea, Aristarchus and Secundus of Thessalonica, Gauis of Derbe, Tychicus and Trophimus of Asia Minor, plus his longtime colleague Timothy (20:4). Luke, who chronicled the Acts of the Apostles, also traveled with Paul at this time (v. 6).

And how had spending time with Paul impacted Timothy? The apostle's own words in 2 Timothy 3:10, "But you have carefully followed my doctrine, manner of life, purpose, faith, long-suffering, love, perseverance," provide a clue.

## THE DANGERS OF DISCIPLING

Are there hazards in the discipling process? Yes, there can be. These dangers can include an inordinate pride in the process of discipling, an abuse of the authority of the role of the discipler and teacher, and the refusal to exercise the spirit of a servant.

In the same Gospel in which Jesus gave the mandate for discipleship, He issued two warnings to counter these dangers. In Matthew 20:25–28, after calling His disciples together, the Lord drew a sharp contrast between their roles and the authority exercised by Gentile rulers and high officials in Israel. Emphatically He declared, "Yet it shall not be so among you." Instead, those who aspired to true greatness must demonstrate a servant's heart. Prominence was to be achieved by being a servant.

The ultimate example, of course, was the Son of Man Himself who came not to be served but to serve and to sacrifice Himself to pay for sins (Matt. 20:28). Later, while sharply criticizing the Pharisaic "teachers of the Law" in Israel who claimed to exercise Moses' authority, Jesus warned,

> "Do not call anyone on earth your father; for One is your Father, He who is in heaven. And do not be called

teachers; for One is your Teacher, the Christ. But he who is greatest among you shall be your servant. And whoever exalts himself will be humbled, and he who humbles himself will be exalted" (Matt. 23:9–12).

The warning is clear. I've seen this happen in modern discipling relationships. The emphasis in discipling should not be to be recognized as skillful disciplers nor have those we disciple make a big issue out of the fact that we are in their particular "discipleship group." I've seen outbreaks of this particular spiritual infection in Bible colleges and seminaries as well as in local churches. Wherever it appears, it's a violation of our Lord's instructions.

Shortly after I became a part of the ministry team at Back to the Bible, our teacher, Woodrow Kroll, and I both received identical copies of a letter from a listener who was extremely concerned because of a small change we'd implemented on the program. In the letter, he called attention to the fact that, on occasion, I had addressed our teacher by his first name, Wood, instead of the more formal Dr. Kroll. He strongly urged that I not refer to "the exalted Bible teacher" in such familiar fashion.

Our goal had been to give our interaction on the program a more personal appeal. I certainly didn't want to create an issue over someone's name or title. I appreciated so much Dr. Kroll's refusal to go along with the listener's insistence on the "status" of a position. His clear-cut response was, "There's only one Person who should be exalted at Back to the Bible—and that's the Lord Jesus Christ."

His response summarizes where discipleship needs to take us. Our purpose is not to make disciples of Woodrow Kroll, myself, or any other Bible teacher. Nor are we interested in developing a core of individuals who consider us to be discipling legends in our own time. Unfortunately when this occurs, the truth is, we've actually become legends in our own minds—and that's the very attitude of pride Jesus rebuked in Matthew 20 and 23.

Instead the Lord's goal for us in the process of discipleship is to move individuals toward the ultimate role model, the One who washed the feet of His followers in John 13, who came not to be served but to serve and to give His life as a ransom for many.

# Chapter Four

# SPOTLIGHT ON THE DISCIPLES

It was a scenario the disciples knew well, since the Passover Feast was something every Jewish family participated in each year. As they went through the familiar rituals, this time in a borrowed upper room in Jerusalem, they must have found themselves increasingly perplexed and distraught.

For three years now they had followed the Man who had become the focal point for their lives, Jesus of Nazareth. Each had responded to the call to follow Him in his own unique way—Matthew from a seat in a tax booth; Nathanael from under a fig tree; Peter, James, and John from their fishing boats.

Over and over they had listened to Him and paid close attention as He taught with self-evident authority in contrast to the style of scribes and Pharisees. At times they must have shaken their heads in puzzled confusion. But they didn't miss the core truth of Jesus' message. He claimed to be the Promised Messiah, the One who would come to call Israel to repentance and bring about the glorious kingdom promised by Moses and the prophets. And He had warned those who listened that unless their righteousness exceeded that of the most religious people of the day—the scribes and Pharisees— they would never become part of that promised kingdom.

Yet these men had done more than simply listen to His message or follow Him. They had embraced Him for who He was—Israel's Messiah. When many who had professed to be His disciples deserted Him, Jesus had asked the Twelve, "Do you also want to go away?" Peter, their acknowledged leader, had responded quickly, "Lord, to whom shall we go? You have the words of eternal life. Also we have come to believe and know that You are the Christ, the Son of the living God" (John 6:68–69).

## TIME TO CHOOSE

This remarkable confession by Peter, undoubtedly reflecting the commitment of the Twelve as a group (with the exception of Judas), happened at a time when Jesus' ministry had become increasingly unpopular with the masses. Many who had been counted among His disciples had begun to struggle with what He was teaching. After He had fed the five thousand, declared Himself to be the Bread of Life, and explained that only those who ate His flesh and drank His blood possessed authentic eternal life, many branded His words "harsh" and unacceptable (6:60). Recognizing the unbelief behind their murmuring, Jesus confronted them with two important truths. First, the fact that they took offense demonstrated their lack of understanding of the true spiritual nature of His message (vv. 61–63). Second, and more to the point, there were some from among the ranks of the disciples who had not trusted in Him (v. 64).

Perhaps as they sat in the Upper Room sharing that fateful Passover meal and listening to Jesus explain that He would be going away from them, some of the Twelve thought back to that earlier day when they had stood with Peter in confessing their solemn allegiance to Jesus as the Messiah, the Son of the living God. They had felt so convinced at that point, so strong in their faith, even in the face of wavering and outright desertion by so many others who had followed the Nazarene.

Now they weren't so sure. "Why can't I follow You now?" Peter asked. "We don't know where You're going, Lord. How can we know the way?" Thomas inquired. Philip requested, "Lord, all we need is to see the Father."

"Lord, how will You demonstrate Yourself to us and not the world?" This from Judas (not Iscariot).

"What does He mean by 'a little while, and you will not see Me and again a little while and you will see Me'?"

Finally, they affirmed, "Now we are sure that You know all things, and have no need that anyone should question You. By this we believe that You came forth from God" (16:30).

## STRENGTHENING THEIR FAITH

But Jesus understood their hearts. He was aware that, like half-cured concrete, their faith still wasn't completely firm. "Do you now believe?" He asked them pointedly (16:31). You're about to desert Me, He warned (v. 32). "Let not your heart be troubled; you believe in God, believe also in Me" (14:1). "Because I have said these things to you, sorrow has filled your heart" (16:6). "You will weep and lament," He explained, "but your sorrow will be turned into joy" (v. 20). "In the world you will have tribulation; but be of good cheer, I have overcome the world" (v. 33).

They had followed Jesus, listened to Him, seen His miracles, accepted Him as Messiah, even anticipated the establishment of His kingdom. Now they couldn't understand what He was telling them. Why was He going away from them and preparing them for grief and trouble?

They must have struggled to understand this special resource He promised, the "Comforter," the Holy Spirit, who would empower them to carry on after He left them (14:16–17). In addition to the presence of the Holy Spirit, He promised them the privilege of instantaneous access to Him by prayer and the promise that their prayers would be answered (vv. 13–14).

He also promised that they would not be left abandoned. He would return to them, confirming the ultimate validity of the faith they had placed in Him (vv. 18–20).

In addition, He promised ample provision for fruitful service, a fruitfulness that would demonstrate the authenticity of their role as His disciples (15:8). This promise was founded on a new and more intimate relationship with Him. They had been servants, unable to understand all the purposes of their master. Now He spoke of them as friends who understand each other's thoughts and hearts (v. 15).

And what did He expect of them in light of their choice to become His disciples? Jesus enumerated several characteristics they were to develop.

His first mandate was obedience. He put it so simply and so plainly that they couldn't miss the point. "If you love Me, keep my commandments" (14:15).

The second mandate was closely tied to the first: Love one another. It was His new commandment to them—that they demonstrate the same love for each other that He had shown them. Such love, beyond doctrine, devotion to duty, or any other single factor, was to become the badge by which all would identity them as His disciples (13:34–35).

They had begun the Passover evening by arguing over who would be greatest, but the Savior had put a stop to that nonsense with a graphic lesson on servanthood, reinforcing His verbal exhortation by playing the role of the lowliest slave and washing their feet in the custom of that day.

The Lord's third mandate was that they bear fruit, lasting fruit that would glorify the name of the Father (15:16).

His fourth mandate was that they not give up in the face of adversity. They would stumble, they would flee. There would be times when they would fail Him—and they could anticipate the same kind of persecution Jesus Himself had faced and would face (vv. 19–20). When they faced adversity, it was crucial that they remember His words (16:4), trust His promise that their sorrow would be turned into unending joy (v. 22), and maintain the kind of close personal relationship with Him that would enable them to experience victory over circumstances and fruitfulness in ministry (15:4).

Finally, it was His goal that they experience the peace of heart and mind that could sustain them in the face of incredible pressures from a hostile world.

As they left the Upper Room and walked through the spring Judean night toward the Garden of Gethsemane, they had been left with two fundamental realities, two essential absolutes—truths that didn't relieve the tension they felt but which helped them face the reality of it. Jesus' final words had been, "In the world you will have tribulation; but be of good cheer, I have overcome the world" (16:33).

What had the Lord been telling them in these final comments before He lifted His eyes to heaven and voiced His prayer to His Father? First, as His disciples they would experience the same pressures and hostilities that He Himself had faced. Yet because of His ultimate victory they, too, would share in the triumph that would become a reality just a few hours later on Easter morning. This final admonition would take on tremendous importance in the hours and days that would follow.

The last thing Jesus would say directly to the Twelve before His prayer to the Father and His confrontation with the mob was "Take courage." What may look like total disaster would ultimately turn into triumph—"I have overcome the world."

According to the gospel records, it was only the second time Jesus had used this word *overcome.* The first time the disciples had heard Him use it, the Pharisees, the source of so much of the hostility against Jesus, had accused the Nazarene of casting out demons by Beelzebub, the prince of demons. Refusing to admit that they were aligned with Satan against Jesus, the Pharisees claimed to be on God's side themselves and accused Jesus of being aligned with Satan.

Jesus had countered by reminding them that a household divided against itself will not stand, and that if He was indeed exercising God's power to cast out demons, this constituted proof that the kingdom of God had penetrated their world of darkness. God had chosen to invade Satan's home turf, and like a strong man, Satan was working to maintain his palace, or to use the modern athletic motif, keep his "home-field advantage" (Luke 4:21).

But now one stronger than Satan had arrived to defeat the Strong Man. The word "overcome," used by Jesus in both Luke 11:21 and John 16:33, is a military term meaning "victory or superiority whether in the physical, legal, or metaphorical sense, whether in mortal conflict or peaceful competition. . . . It is generally assumed that a *nikaw* [Greek for victory or conquest] . . . is demonstrated by an action, by the overthrow of the opposing force and that the success is palpable and manifest to all eyes."[1]

It must have seemed in those final Upper Room moments that Jesus was giving His disciples the ultimate challenge to faith. They would see Him taken before their very eyes, find themselves fleeing in terror, then watch Him being nailed to a cross to die like a common criminal. Only after their dramatic encounter with an empty tomb and a risen Savior would they begin to understand the impact of His words, "Take courage, I have overcome the world."

It was the ultimate gift of Jesus to His Twelve and to each of us who would be His disciples today. We find ourselves playing on a hostile field, against a powerful foe, and in front of a hostile crowd, but we have been guaranteed the final victory. Jesus Himself secured the ultimate victory when He cried out from the cross, "It is finished."

## THE CALLING OF THE TWELVE

To learn more about these disciples and the role they played, it will help us to step back in time to examine some of the watershed events in their experiences with Jesus. The first happened early in Jesus' ministry. Crowds had been following the Master, and miracles were occurring. Jesus had called a small group of disciples to follow Him. Peter and Andrew had responded to the call one day as they cast their nets into the sea (Mark 1:16–18). James and John, who were nearby mending their nets, also responded immediately (vv. 19–20). A short time later, Matthew, the tax collector, left his lucrative occupation to follow Jesus. He even threw a party to celebrate his new commitment and to introduce his associates to the One to whom he had given allegiance (2:13–16).

Yet opposition to Jesus had begun to build as the Pharisees challenged the disciples' behavior (v. 24) and scrutinized Jesus' actions so they could bring Him down (3:1–2). They had even huddled with their archrivals the Herodians—it was the equivalent of a caucus between liberal Democrats and conservative Republicans—to find a way to destroy the One they perceived to be their common enemy.

In the face of this opposition Jesus undertook the first of His withdrawals (v. 7). Crowds from all over Palestine followed, a vast assortment of individuals who were curious about the miracles He was performing (vv. 7–8). Many of them had seen one or more of His miraculous deeds (vv. 10–11).

Yet Jesus was after much more than the adulation of those who were curious about the nature of His power. He chose to focus on those who were convinced of the truth of His claims to be the Messiah, the Son of God, and who would commit to following Him whatever the cost.

So after a night of consultation with His Father, He called the ones He wanted to be with Him and to send forth to serve Him (vv. 13–14). By this time at least seventy individuals could have been loosely considered His disciples, perhaps even hundreds. From this larger group, Jesus carefully selected twelve. They would be the starters on His team, the ones who would take the field following His death and resurrection and go into action on the Day of Pentecost.

From today's perspective, we might expect Jesus to have carefully gone over the résumés of all His potential followers, interviewed them utilizing the latest assessment techniques, perhaps even subjected them to a battery of psychological and vocational tests. In reality He did nothing of the kind. In fact, the only individual Jesus consulted regarding the choice of these men was His Father in heaven.

Many years ago I came across a tongue-in-cheek memorandum from the Jordan Management Consultants in Jerusalem to Jesus, Son of Joseph, at the Woodcrafters Carpenter Shop in Nazareth. The letter read as follows:

Dear Sir:

Thank you for submitting the résumés of the twelve men you've picked for managerial positions in your new organization. All of them have now taken our battery of tests, and we have not only run the results through our computer but also arranged personal interviews for each of them with our psychologist and vocational aptitude consultant. The profiles of all tests are included, and you will want to study each of them carefully.

It is the staff opinion that most of your nominees are lacking in background, education, and vocational aptitude for the type of enterprise you are undertaking. They do not have a team concept. We would recommend that you continue your search for persons of experience in managerial ability and proven capability.

Simon Peter is emotionally unstable and given to fits of temper. Andrew has absolutely no qualities of leadership. The two brothers, James and John, the sons of Zebedee, place personal interest above company loyalty. Thomas demonstrates a questioning attitude that would tend to undermine morale. We feel it our duty to tell you that Matthew has been blacklisted by the Greater Jerusalem Business Bureau. James, the son of Alphaeus, and Thaddeus definitely have radical leanings, and they both registered a high score on the manic-depressive scale.

One of the candidates, however, shows great potential. He is a man of ability and resourcefulness, meets people well, has a keen business mind, and has contacts in high places. He is highly motivated, ambitious, and responsible. We recommend Judas Iscariot as your controller and right-hand man. All of the other profiles are self-explanatory.

We wish you every success in your new venture.

Sincerely,

Jordan Management Consultants

## Marked by Weaknesses

There is a sense in which, even though we may chuckle in response to this humorous attempt to read twentieth-century personnel techniques into a first-century process, we can't help but see the kernel of truth reflected by this letter. After all, Jesus clearly chose individuals with significant deficiencies.

### Lacking in Faith

For one thing, they were seriously lacking in faith. It's a weakness that surfaced early in the disciples' career, shortly after Jesus responded to the pressing crowds by withdrawing (Matt. 8:18) and by seeking to refine the commitment of some of His weaker followers (8:19–22).

Entering a boat on the Sea of Galilee, Jesus led His core disciples, many of whom were experienced fishermen, into the teeth of a massive storm. Unintimidated by the elements, He slept in the boat until His men awakened Him, pleading "Lord, save us. We are perishing" (8:25). His response pinpointed their critical deficiency. Controlled by fear, they were sadly lacking in faith.

Many years ago I drove a Volkswagon, one of the original "Beetles" that used to be so common on our highways back in the sixties and seventies. It was extremely economical to operate, and it handled very well. But my little bug had one major deficiency—it just didn't have the horsepower to pass anything moving faster than a horse and buggy. Like the disciples' faith, it was a car of little horsepower.

### Lacking in Insight

Not only were they lacking in faith, the disciples were also deficient in insight. In Matthew 13 the Lord unfolded the mysteries of the kingdom of heaven in a series of seven parables. Since they would be the ones to carry the message of this kingdom following His time on earth, He followed His presentation with a question we might easily have anticipated: "Have you understood all these things?" (v. 51). We aren't surprised at their collective reply, "Yes, Lord. Right! We got it! No problem, Jesus. We can handle it."

Knowing their hearts and realizing that they thought they understood much more than they actually did, Jesus shared another private parable—it's been called the eighth in a series of seven. They had asked no questions, expressed no reservations. In fact, they might have been able to deliver a sermon or a discourse on the soils, the wheat and the tares, the leaven, or the pearl of great price. Like many of us today, they had a handle on what the symbols meant and understood the language Jesus had used. But they still hadn't put it all together. The Lord wanted them to move beyond a mere grasp of the facts to true insight. So He told a three-step anecdote: study like a scribe, exercise the self-discipline of a householder, and put it together like someone on a treasure hunt.

In some ways the disciples were like many of us today who give casual attention to the study of the Word but never immerse ourselves in diligently digging into its depths for life-changing truth.

What Jesus wanted to see in them was a heart like that of Ezra, who had been described as "a skilled scribe in the Law of Moses" (Ezra 7:6). Now a scribe was first a student, a man who carefully dug into the text to find out what it said. As a result, he became able to give an accurate and authoritative interpretation of the Word. Ezra's ministry, which highlighted the necessity of rebuilding the walls of Jerusalem, focused first on rebuilding the hearts and minds of people through a commitment to studying and applying the Word.

How does a ready scribe operate? Ezra himself described the threefold process in Ezra 7:10, "For Ezra had prepared his heart to seek the Law of the Lord, and to do it, and to teach statutes and ordinances in Israel."

First, Ezra had committed himself to seeking out God's Law, discovering what it says, and coming to grasp with what it means. This same process is essential for us to experience lives that reflect biblical principles. As my colleague Woodrow Kroll recently said at one of Back to the Bible's Life Insights Seminars, "It's no wonder we have trouble applying God's Word today. Many of us haven't taken the time to find out what it says or what it means."

Once we understand what the text says and means, then we're in a position to apply it, to do what it says, to fulfill its mandates the way Ezra did. This in turn prepares us to communicate God's truth to others, helping them understand how to apply principles from God's Word to every situation and to develop skill at living "by the Book."

The disciples not only needed a scribe's aptitude for study, they also needed the self-discipline of a householder. Jesus' second metaphor pictures the individual who is in charge of overseeing a household, the basic building block of society, in the world of Jesus' day. The word Jesus used for a "householder" is not the common "steward," but another related term that literally means "the house despot." It seems to me that Jesus' use of this word underscored the importance of self-discipline. It is interesting to note the obvious connection between the terms *discipline* and *disciple*. They go together like a hand and glove.

The third process Jesus sought to implement in correcting His disciples' insight deficiency was integration. According to the master, the householder brings treasures both old and new. That's exactly what Jesus had been doing for His disciples, presenting truths they were well aware of—the messianic kingdom—and others they didn't know about—that it would also include elements of evil, and that good and evil would coexist under the professed "banner" of Jesus' followers. Clearly He wanted them to develop the insight to "put it all together."

Unfortunately the disciples still hadn't learned to put it all together. According to Mark 6:52, the hardness of their hearts kept them from grasping the significance of the incredible power Jesus had demonstrated when He fed the five thousand, walked on the water, and stilled the storm.

### Lacking in Power

In addition to these deficiencies in faith and insight, the disciples also lacked the power for effective ministry. In Matthew 17, following that incredible transfiguration experience, Peter, James, and John returned with Jesus to discover the father of an epileptic son begging the Master to heal his son. "I brought him to Your disciples, but they could not cure him" (Matt. 17:16). Why the lack of power? Jesus told them plainly, "Because of your unbelief" (v. 20). Despite their time with Jesus, they were still more like the "faithless and perverse generation" to whom they had been ministering (v. 17).

### Lacking in Humility

Despite these major gaps in character, the disciples weren't lacking in self-confidence, even though they clearly lacked humility. There is perhaps no better example of their confidence than an incident that occurred as Jesus and His disciples were en route to Jerusalem. The Lord had just spelled out the full details of what was about to happen—His betrayal, His death by crucifixion, and His resurrection on the third day.

Almost immediately following this explanation, Salome, the mother of James and John, approached Jesus with a bold request, "Grant that these two sons of mine may sit, one on Your right hand and the other on the left, in Your kingdom" (Matt. 20:21).

We often see contemporary parents whose agendas for their sons and daughters come into conflict with what the Lord wants in their lives. So it's no surprise to see it happen with some of Jesus' men.

Now it's impossible for us to tell whether this request was related to the fact that theirs was apparently a fairly well-to-do family. After all, Zebedee had hired servants who helped with the fishing business, owned a house in Jerusalem, and was known as a friend of the High Priest Caiaphas and his household. Perhaps it isn't surprising that those who had enjoyed a measure of relative wealth and the benefits of connection with influential people should demand choice positions in the kingdom. However, such ambitions weren't limited to the family of Zebedee.

There were numerous occasions when this issue had surfaced. A short time before, the disciples had come to Jesus to ask who would be greatest in the kingdom of heaven. It was a topic of frequent discussion among them (Mark 9:33–37; Luke 9:46–48), and at times the issue erupted into out-and-out conflict (Luke 22:24; Matt. 23:11). Ironically, this strife took place as the disciples sat in the Upper Room, perhaps just before Jesus' inescapable demonstration of true servanthood when He washed their feet. So while these men Jesus had called to Himself lacked humility, they certainly didn't seem to lack brash self-confidence.

### Lacking in Perseverance

One final deficiency was recorded by Matthew: These men lacked commitment, or what we might call perseverance or staying power. When crunch time arrived, when they saw the Master arrested and taken away, Matthew doesn't hesitate to tell the shameful truth: "Then all the disciples forsook Him and fled" (Matt. 26:56).

Ironically, only a short time earlier they had all joined Peter in affirming, "Even if I have to die with You, I will not deny You" (v. 35). What they lacked in steadfastness, they made up in brash self-confidence. "No problem, Lord. We can handle it." But they were tragically wrong.

### PROFILES OF RELUCTANCE

Following World War II, a former naval officer from Massachusetts who had served on a navy patrol boat in the Pacific wrote a book entitled *Profiles in Courage.* Now, anyone looking at the record of Jesus' disciples in the New Testament would never have written a book about them bearing a title even remotely similar to the book written by John F. Kennedy. Certainly they had their strong points.

But no one honestly scanning this list of men would con-
fuse them with the cream of the crop. They were ordinary
people just like you and me, people with struggles, flaws,
and deficiencies.

Yet they were the men Jesus called to Himself, invested
time in. He put them through the process, then sent them
forth to change their world forever. Let's consider them
individually.

*Peter*

Any discussion of the disciples almost has to begin with
Peter. You could probably end with him as well. In fact
Herbert Lockyer in his excellent book *All the Men of the Bible*
suggests that Peter would require "a book all his own to fully
expand his life and labors."[2]

One of the original followers of John the Baptist, Peter
had been invited to Jesus by his brother Andrew. Apparently
they had been fishing in partnership with the two sons of
Zebedee on the lake of Galilee.

Peter's finer points included a frank humility, demonstrated when he responded to the first miracle he saw Jesus
do with the words, "Depart from me, for I am a sinful man,
O Lord!" (Luke 5:8). Often quick to grasp spiritual truth—
witness his confessions of Christ's divinity and messiahship
in John 6:68 and Matthew 16:16—yet he could also speak
for Satan (Matt. 16:22–23). He often demonstrated an impulsive lack of understanding of what Jesus was trying to
teach, as he did on the Mount of Transfiguration (Mark 9:5–
6). Mark's description—probably received from Peter himself—demonstrated the reality of what was going on in the
mind of the big fisherman. He spoke his suggestion that they
build three tabernacles because he really didn't know what
to say (v. 6). Furthermore, he and his two companions were
overcome by fear (v. 6).

Here's a man we can identify with, a man confronted with
something outside the box, totally beyond the realm of his
experience—and he's frightened to death. Not knowing
what to say, he blurts out the first thing that comes to mind,
what initially must have seemed like a good idea. Then Peter was interrupted by the voice of God the Father saying,
"This is My beloved Son. Hear Him!" (v. 7).

Peter's courageous and insightful confessions (Matt. 16:16–17; John 6:68) marked him as spokesman and leader of the Twelve. Ironically, although all the disciples fled, he was the only one who openly denied the Lord (Mark 14:68, 70–72).

Impulsive, he had been the one who walked on water (Matt. 14:28) and who plunged into the lake of Galilee when he spotted Jesus on the shore (John 21:7).

Yet this prototypical disciple ultimately grew from a man marked by inconsistency, impulsiveness, and overblown self-confidence to a courageous preacher, a leader in the early church, a man whose final words called on Christ's followers to "grow in the grace and knowledge of our Lord and Savior Jesus Christ" (2 Peter 3:16). According to tradition, he died by crucifixion, "nailed to a cross upside down because he considered himself unworthy to die in the same way his Lord had."[3]

### James and John

Clearly associated with Peter in what seems to have been an "inner circle" were James and John, fishermen and sons of a wealthy father and an ambitious mother. Their angry reaction to an inhospitable Samaritan village—"Lord, do You want us to command fire to come down from heaven and consume them?" (Luke 9:54–56)—gave credence to their nickname "sons of thunder." They had been aware of their mother's presumptuous request for chief seats in the kingdom of heaven (Mark 10:35); in effect, their presence added a "Yeah, Lord, can we?"

Yet James ultimately became one of the leaders in the early church and had the privilege of being one of the first martyrs for the faith (Acts 12:2).

John, James' younger brother, was labeled "the disciple whom Jesus loved." He sat next to Christ in the Upper Room, was given the privilege of caring for Jesus' mother, Mary, when the Savior hung on the cross. John was perhaps the closest to Jesus, humanly speaking, of all the disciples.

The fact that he lived until he was almost one hundred, far longer than the other disciples, and the way Jesus treated him almost like a son, indicated that John may have been the youngest of the Twelve. Through his epistles he played a leading role in shaping the belief and practice of the early church. During his exile to the rocky island of Patmos, he was given the incredible and detailed unfolding of the climactic prophetic events of history in what we call the book of the Revelation.

### Andrew

Then there was Andrew, Peter's brother. He had been listening to John the Baptist when his life was changed forever. John had spotted Jesus and pointed Him out as the Lamb of God who takes away the sin of the world (John 1:29). Andrew immediately began following Jesus—John even recorded that it happened the tenth hour of the day (v. 39). Immediately Andrew began doing what he has perhaps become best known for—bringing others to Jesus. Hurrying to his older brother, he invited Peter to the Savior and thus became the spiritual grandfather to all those multitudes Peter fathered in the faith. Later, Andrew would invite a young lad to bring his lunch and come to Jesus (6:8–9), and on another occasion he brought a group of Greek-speaking Jews who had come seeking Jesus.

In his three appearances in the Gospels other than the "roster of the Twelve," Andrew was involved each time in pointing someone to the Savior. Rumor has it that, like his brother Peter, Andrew ultimately suffered crucifixion because of his faith.

### Philip

Like Peter and Andrew, Philip was a native of Bethsaida in Galilee who first met Jesus in his home town (1:43–44). Unlike them, he waited until Jesus invited him to join the company of followers. Ironically, the name Philip—which means lover of horses—was Greek, even though he was Jewish. In the lists of disciples, Philip is linked with Nathanael, who was probably his best friend. "We have found Him of whom Moses in the law, and also the prophets, wrote—Jesus of Nazareth, the son of Joseph," he insisted (v. 45). When his friend expressed skepticism, Philip demanded, "Come and see" (v. 46).

His practical, conservative bent and cautious manner caused Philip to struggle at the feeding of the five thousand when Jesus asked for his suggestion (6:5–7). "Two hundred denarii worth of bread is not sufficient for them, that every one of them may have a little." had been his reply. Later he wound up having to call on Andrew to figure out how to handle those Greek-speaking seekers (12:21). His continued struggle with faith came to a head in the Upper Room when he urged Jesus, "Show us the Father and it is sufficient for us." Jesus' reply pointed out how long the process of growth took with Philip and the others. "Have I been with you so long, and yet you have not known Me, Philip? He who has seen Me has seen the Father" (14:8–9).

### Nathanael

Philip's friend Nathanael (also believed to be Bartholomew), the dreamer or visionary, was almost the opposite of Philip the pragmatist. Introduced as Bartholomew in three of the Gospels, but apparently the same man John identifies as Nathanael, he initially expresses a degree of prejudice and skepticism, "Can anything good come out of Nazareth?" But as Jesus pointed out, "Behold and Israelite, in whom is no deceit!" (1:47). When Nathanael skeptically responded, "How do you know me?" Jesus pointed out, "Before Philip called you, when you were under the fig tree, I saw you" (v. 48). Nathanael's response was immediate. Acknowledging the Lord as "Rabbi," he confessed his faith in Jesus as God's Son and Israel's Messiah, and the Lord promised him even greater insights for the days ahead.

### Matthew

The next disciple on Jesus' list, Matthew, was also known by the name Levi. His occupation, tax collector, caused him to be hated by almost everyone in Israel, where men of his calling ranked even lower than IRS agents or lawyers in modern society. It wouldn't have been surprising if people had stood on the street corners of Jerusalem and exchanged "publican jokes" in much the same manner that people tell lawyer jokes today.

Matthew's call to discipleship came as he sat at the tax booth in Capernaum, which may have been the most cosmopolitan city in Palestine at that time. His response was immediate. According to Luke, he arose from his seat, followed Jesus, and abandoned everything (Luke 5:28). It was an immediate, decisive, and total response that even led to a new endeavor (Mark 2:15). He threw a party—today we might call it an evangelistic dinner—inviting his former associates to meet the One who had given his life new meaning and direction. Perhaps Matthew's greatest legacy for followers of Christ was his Gospel with its focus on the king and the kingdom, a term he used more than fifty times in his narrative of the life of Christ.

### Thomas

Thomas was also known as Didymus, "the twin." Some have suggested that his first name was Judas, the same as two of the other disciples. Others have suggested that the name Didymus hinted at his "double-minded" character. When Jesus expressed his resolve to return to Judea, Thomas was the one who suggested, "Let us also go, that we may die with Him" (John 11:16). This curt remark demonstrated both his pessimism and his resolve. Later, in the Upper Room, he expressed a profound misunderstanding of what Jesus was explaining. "Lord, we do not know where You are going, and how can we know the way?" (14:5).

Yet Thomas is probably best remembered for his post-resurrection skepticism. He alone had been absent when Christ first appeared to the disciples as a group in that Upper Room—and he wasn't about to take their word for what had happened (20:28). The following week the Lord immediately and graciously gave Thomas the evidence he requested (21:2). Without hesitation, the twin reaffirmed his faith—a faith based on eyewitness evidence. Yet Jesus pointed out that those who haven't seen and still believe experience an even greater measure of blessing than had Thomas.

### James, the Son of Alphaeus

James, the son of Alphaeus, is commonly referred to as James the Less, or "the little," perhaps because of his shortness of stature. The only information Scripture gives about him is the name of his father and his designation as the "the little one."

### Thaddeus

Judas or Thaddeus also occupied a less prominent role in the Gospel records. His one solo part occurs in the Upper Room when he asked, "Lord, how is it that You will manifest Yourself to us, and not to the world?" (14:22).

### Simon

Simon the Zealot is another of the lesser-known disciples. Apparently he was a member of a radically conservative Jewish political party, zealots who loved the land and did everything in their power to disrupt foreign interference, especially Roman dominion. Apparently Simon the Zealot transferred his zeal and commitment from his previous life to the Master, and found ultimate freedom in the One who said, "If the Son makes you free, you will be free indeed."

### Judas Iscariot

The final disciple in the list, Judas Iscariot, stands out as one of the ultimate enigmas of both Scripture and history. Why did Jesus choose him to be part of the Twelve? The only answer that makes any sense is the one Matthew gives, "That the Scriptures of the prophets might be fulfilled" (Matt. 26:56). After all, the psalmist had predicted a terrible act of betrayal centuries before (Ps. 109:5–8), and the prophet Zachariah had even predicted the bargain price—thirty pieces of silver (Zach. 11:12–13).

Frequently labeled the betrayer, Judas was also identified by Jesus in His prayer to the Heavenly Father as the son of perdition (John 17:12). Later, Paul would give the same designation to the man of sin, the individual we commonly refer to as the Antichrist (2 Thess. 2:3).

Judas was also a thief. Chosen by the disciples as treasurer, he obviously received more trust than he warranted. Frequently his materialistic nature surfaced in the New Testament. John recorded one such incident, noting Judas' complaint when Mary took a pound of costly ointment to anoint Jesus' feet. "Why was this fragant oil not sold for three hundred denarii and given to the poor?" he piously asked (John 12:5). Then John carefully recorded his observations about Judas' character: He cared nothing for the poor, and though he was the trusted treasurer he was also a thief (17:6).

Perhaps the ultimate example of Judas' hypocrisy occurred when he betrayed the Master with a kiss, the classic way of greeting a friend (Matt. 26:48–49).

Yet even at that critical moment of betrayal Jesus addressed him as "friend" (v. 50). Earlier in the Upper Room He'd extended to Judas the "sop," the evidence of honor, apparently continuing to hold out the opportunity for the son of perdition to turn from his betrayal.

What an incredible life Judas led! He began with such potential—chosen to be one of the Twelve by Jesus, trusted as treasurer by the disciples.

Yet his career was marked by a continued rejection of the truth to which he was exposed. "For everyone to whom much is given, from him much will be required," Jesus had said (Luke 12:48). And Judas failed to utilize the vast amount of truth he was given. His growing cynicism, his materialistic dishonesty, and his utter hypocrisy stand as a solemn warning to all those who give profession of allegiance to the Savior today. Here was a man who undoubtedly could impress any church, Christian organization, or ministry, yet he ultimately ended up a tragic failure and a suicide.

## JUST LIKE US

So these were the men Jesus chose to be with Him, to follow Him and learn from Him. From the record of their behavior in the Gospels it's hard to see how they would ultimately become giants of the faith. Yet that's exactly what happened. They were people like you and like me, with the same kinds of struggles we experience, the same kinds of failures, inconsistencies, and flaws. Take the time to look over their record again, become more familiar with them individually and as a group.

Ask yourself, "Aren't they just like me?"

Then take it a step further. If Christ could use these men to turn the world upside down, think of what He can do if we are willing to become His disciples. Ordinary men—that's what they were. Yet, they became obedient, humble, submissive. They developed a concern for each other. They finally learned those lessons of selfless commitment and ultimately became real heroes.

## NEEDED: HEROES

Heroes—that's what our society needs today. In a world of commercially made heroes like Michael Jordan, antiheroes like O. J. Simpson, or nonheroes like Bart Simpson, we need true heroes in contrast to the fake heroes of our day—Batman, the Mighty Morphin Power Rangers, or Ninja Turtles. We need authentic heroes, genuine role models. According to Irvin Rien, Professor of Communications at Northwestern University in Evanston, Illinois, our society today has confused heroes with celebrities. "Making someone well-known is now a professional business. The distribution channels of radio and TV overwhelm us. We're constantly faced with input from Michael Jackson, O. J. Simpson, Terry Bradshaw, Tommy Lee Jones. People begin to know the celebrity better than they know their own family."[4] According to Rien, this shift began in the 1920s when the concept of celebrity began appearing in the press and when athletes like Babe Ruth and Ty Cobb appeared on the scene.

Yet Dr. Rien recognizes that society does need models. But what kind of models do we need? Models who are human, yes—models who struggle as we do, whether they're larger than life like Peter or relatively obscure like Philip. But above all, we need heroes who are ordinary people.

In December of 1994 Ellen College in North Carolina held what was billed as "Local Heroes Day."[5] Five area residents were chosen by the freshmen class to be labeled heroes. Their qualifications? A sustained commitment to moral ideals, a disposition to act in accord with those ideals, a willingness to sacrifice, a tendency to be inspiring, and a sense of realistic humility.

Ironically, those same traits can be seen in the lives of the twelve men Jesus discipled, the men who ultimately turned their world upside down for Him.

## ENDNOTES

1. Gerhard Kittel, ed., *Theological Dictionary of the New Testament,* vol. 4 (Grand Rapids: Eerdmans, 1967), 942.
2. Herbert Lockyer, *All the Men of the Bible* (Grand Rapids: Zondervan, 1958), 272.
3. Ibid., 273.
4. *The Lincoln Star,* 31 January 1995, 4.
5. Ibid.

# PART TWO

# DISCIPLING: CHRIST'S APPROACH

B uilding a house is an exciting project. So is constructing a church building. I've had the privilege of being
involved in both.

When we constructed a new building at the church I
pastored in Louisiana, our six acres was located in what was,
for all practical purposes, a swamp. The man from whom
we secured the property promised to bring the land up to a
certain grade level. He figured it would take twenty dump
trucks filled with dirt. It ultimately took over two hundred!

It seemed that the process of preparing the foundation
took forever. But finally the time came when all the dirt was
spread in place, the foundation was poured, and we were
ready to go up with the framework.

Our foundation has been laid, and we are prepared to look
at the framework, the steps Jesus took in discipling His men.
Remember, these steps are taken from our Lord's our words
in John 17, steps that detail exactly what He did.

Before we move into this section, let me make two observations: First, the disciples are clearly at the heart of Jesus'
prayer to the Father. More than forty times in this prayer the
Master made reference to His men. As He speaks to the Father, He sees the world through the twelve men He raised up.

Second, even though He gives us such a clear outline of how the process of discipleship worked in the relationship between Him and His twelve, His focus is not on discipleship. Rather, what seems to be uppermost in His mind as He talks with His Father is an essential concept found throughout Scripture. It is reflected in the words "I have glorified You on the earth. I have finished the work which You have given me to do" (John 17:4).

The theme of glorifying the Father is a prominent one in John's gospel. The verb *to glorify* appears seventeen times in these 21 chapters, and five of these are found in chapter 17. The noun *glory* can be found eleven times in the gospel, three in Jesus' prayer to His Father.

Throughout John's gospel the glorifying of Jesus is tied to what He calls "the hour." Frequently He emphasized that His "hour" had not yet come (2:4; 7:30; 8:20). Finally in John 12:23, when the Greek-speaking seekers are brought to Jesus, He responds by saying, "The hour has come that the Son of Man should be glorified."

Immediately the Lord made three statements that connect the concepts of His hour and glorification to His death and His ministry of discipling. First He used the example of a grain of wheat that falls into the ground and dies to show why His death was necessary for Him to multiply and bear fruit (v. 24). Then he pointed out the importance of commitment on the part of those who would follow Him, a commitment that transcends any ties of people or things of this life (vv. 25–26). Finally, He noted that this "hour," though bringing Him great agony of soul, was the very purpose for which He had come to earth. At that point He called out, "Glorify Your name" (v. 28), and the Father's voice from heaven replied, "I have both glorified it and will glorify it again."

This same emphasis becomes a strategic part of Jesus' prayer to the Father in John 17. In fact, His explanation of how discipleship works is really a by-product of His explanation of how He glorified the Father. Clearly the emphasis in John 17 is on glory, as eight times He uses a form of the word—twice in verse one.

The concept of glory comes from the Old Testament term *cavad,* which means "of heavy weight." The picture conveyed by this word is consistent with valuable metals and priceless jewels. The heavier they are, the more glorious.

Gold or jewelry of higher carat weight will generally have more value than that of lesser weight. We see something of this concept in the mind of the apostle Paul as he wrote to the Corinthian church to contrast his present suffering with the "eternal weight of glory" to be anticipated (2 Cor. 4:17). The word *doxa*, used some 280 times in the New Testament, carried the basic idea of reputation, power, and the divine mode of being.[1] Throughout the book of John the concept was used interchangeably of Jesus and God the Father, thus strongly reinforcing the deity of Christ. Indeed John begins His gospel with a clear-cut statement that Jesus, the incarnate Word, lived in our midst to give us the opportunity to behold His glory, the glory of the only begotten of the Father, full of grace and truth. John writes, "No one has seen God at any time. The only begotten Son, who is in the bosom of the Father, He has declared Him" (1:18).

This declaration provides an important insight into the message of John 17—the statements Jesus made about what He had done, plus a corresponding principle to apply.

First, God's major purpose, consistent with His perfect character and being, is to manifest His own glory. Being the self-existent God that He is, this is both right and reasonable. In fact, the primary passion of Jesus on earth, both in His life and through His death, was to glorify the Father. As He lifts His face to heaven, recognizing that the momentous hour had arrived, His primary passion is "Glorify Your Son, that Your Son also may glorify You" (v. 1). He recognized that He had finished one aspect of the work He has been given to do, which has brought glory to the Father (v. 4). Now another phase is about to begin, which will conclude with the Father exalting the Son to the same glorious position He occupied before creation (v. 5). In addition Jesus says, "I am glorified in them [the disciples]" (v. 10), "And the glory which You gave Me I have given them" (v. 22), and "Father, I desire that they also whom You gave Me may be with Me where I am, that they may behold My glory which You have given Me" (v. 24).

So how does this manifestation of God's glory affect the process of master discipleship? Ultimately the Lord's emphasis moves beyond discipling to the ultimate goal of this and all worthy endeavors—bringing glory to God. This is reflected in the summary statement of everything Jesus had done regarding these men, "I have declared to them Your Name, and will declare it, that the love with which You loved Me may be in them and I in them" (v. 26). Without question, the process of discipleship leads to a greater grasp and appreciation of God, a closer relationship with Him, a greater understanding of the sum total of His attributes as reflected in His name. This in turn leads to a greater measure of love, the badge of discipleship, and a greater experiencing of the empowering reflected in the indwelling Christ, who is the vine to every fruitful branch.

It's an important principle for us to keep in mind. Our final goal isn't the process of discipleship or even a product—disciples. The ultimate objective is to glorify the Father and His Son.

## ENDNOTE

1.  Kittel, *Theological Dictionary*, vol. 2, 247.

Chapter Five

---

# DISCIPLESHIP STEP 1:
# EXAMPLE

"I manifested Your name to the men
whom You have given Me" (John 17:6).

Some time ago I was invited by Southeastern Bible College, from which I graduated many years ago, to present a series of chapel messages on the subject of ministry in the nineties. The topic I had been assigned forced me to step back, reflect on some twenty-five years of my own ministry, and wrestle with the question of what constitutes successful ministry today.

For some people successful ministry in the nineties might involve using the latest technology. Within the past week at least two of my colleagues at Back to the Bible have taken advantage of opportunities to share the Gospel while surfing the Internet. Another friend of mine, the CEO of a major Christian-oriented corporation, is involved in starting a new business designed to provide a distinctively Christian on-line service, a counterpart to Prodigy, America Online, and similar services.

Technology today is remarkable. Just last week I talked with one of the executives of Trans World Radio about a project they had developed with HCJB in Quito, Ecuador, a satellite and computer system for delivering Christian programs to radio stations in Latin America digitally, storing them in a computer hard drive, then calling them up for broadcast at the time they are scheduled to air. This new technology, not yet even available in the United States, represents a quantum leap from the days when programs like *Back to the Bible* were shipped by mail on large reels of magnetic tape, and before that on vinyl disks to be played on turntables.

Others believe successful ministry in the nineties involves getting a handle on the latest methods, statistics, and marketing strategies. The church we were involved in for many years in suburban Dallas began with fifty people in a bait shop near the shores of Lake Ray Hubbard, just east of the Dallas-Fort Worth metroplex. In ten years it grew to a thriving assembly of more than two thousand worshipers on an average weekend, and almost 90 percent of the growth came from conversions rather than transfers. According to the founding pastor, the key was the church's mission to produce fully developing followers of Christ in the Lake Ray Hubbard area by using a seeker-sensitive ministry designed to attract the unchurched and unsaved. Similar success stories of rapidly growing assemblies and even mega-churches can be seen in other places in North America. Meanwhile, seminars to present principles of church growth or understanding baby boomers, busters, and generation Xers have proliferated like umbrellas on a sun-drenched beach.

### STARTING POINT FOR SUCCESSFUL MINISTRY

As I wrestled with the concept of successful ministry in the nineties, I found myself driven back to the one book in the New Testament that has more to say on the subject of ministry than any other, Paul's second letter to the Corinthians, an epistle that reflects the anguish of his heart and the tears in his eyes. The beleaguered apostle wrote to defend his approach to ministry, which had come under sharp criticism and attack by the very Corinthians to whom he sought to minister. The apostle began by talking about encouragement, one of the major themes throughout 2 Corinthians, describing God as the Father of mercies—the God who feels our pain—and the God of all encouragement, who is there for us, called alongside to help in every time of trouble (2 Cor. 1:3–4). Recognizing that his own adversity has given him opportunity to minister to others, Paul candidly shared the trouble he experienced in Asia Minor—a time when the pressures went so far beyond what he could handle that he didn't expect to survive (v. 8). Yet God used that adversity to strengthen Paul's trust (v. 9), and the Corinthians' prayer and assistance, along with that of other believers, gave him cause for thanksgiving (v. 11).

Yet Paul had clearly come under attack by some from among the Corinthians. They had been upset because he had changed his travel plans after letting them know he planned to stop over on his way to Macedonia and on his return trip to Judea. From his initial ministry defense (vv. 12–2:4) it appears the Corinthians had accused him of treating them in cavalier fashion, telling them he planned to visit them, then doing something else. Such vacillation, they charged, brought his preaching ministry into question, not to mention the issue of whether he really cared about them or just wanted to lord it over them.

So how did Paul defend his ministry? He didn't say a thing about his methods or the technology he may have taken advantage of or the statistical results of his labors. No, those were not the emphases of his ministry.

That's what I discovered as I considered the question of ministry in the nineties. If somehow we could set up a satellite teleconferencing link between earth and heaven and invite the apostle Paul to lecture us on the subject of effective ministry for our day and time, I believe he would start with us right where he began his defense to the Corinthians.

> For our boasting is this: the testimony of our conscience that we conducted ourselves in the world in simplicity and godly sincerity, not with fleshly wisdom, but by the grace of God, and more abundantly toward you (2 Cor. 1:12).

Where did Paul begin? By talking about integrity, example, and personal conduct. That, I believe, is where any discussion of effective ministry for our day must begin.

When Paul talked about ministry, he didn't start with methods or techniques. In fact, he didn't even begin by calling for a clear, consistent message—even though this was obviously a major concern as he indicated when he warned

Timothy to "preach the Word" (2 Tim. 4:2). Before he ever told Timothy to preach the Word, Paul warned his young protégé "to be an example to the believers in word, in conduct, in love, in spirit, in faith, in purity" (1 Tim. 4:12).

Furthermore, as he warned Timothy to preach the Word in the dangerous days in which he lived, Paul reminded the young man he mentored, "But you have carefully followed my doctrine, manner of life, purpose, faith, longsuffering, love, perseverance, persecutions . . ." (2 Tim. 3:10–11).

Paul described the day in which he lived as one in which "evil men and imposters will grow worse, deceiving and being deceived" (v. 13). To counter this evil influence, Timothy was to follow both the example and the teaching of his mentor, Paul (v. 14).

Here I believe is the starting point, the foundational step in discipling, the one on which all other steps ultimately rest. It is the step of example. Jesus stated, "I have manifested Your Name to the men whom You have given Me out the world" (John 17:6).

I recall being attracted to the ministry of the man who mentored me in the faith, Alden Gannett, because of his clear, powerful preaching. I loved his ministry of the Word, and when as a teenager I sensed God's call in my life to vocational ministry, I decided I wanted the training to be able to preach the Word like he did.

However, his godly example was of equal importance in the influence he had on my life during my high school and my college years. I became close friends with two of his sons, Keith and Ron, and since we attended the same church, I frequently found myself in their home. Dr. Gannett's godly testimony, a walk that backed up his message, plus the cheerful spirit of his wife, Georgetta, greatly impacted my life.

I saw a man who demonstrated patience with people in a variety of trying circumstances, who had a passion for God, and who radiated authentic humility.

## RESPONSIBILITY FOR MODELING

It is not inconsequential that Antioch was where the disciples came to be called Christians. Under the watchful encouragement and ministry of Barnabas and Paul, the believers flourished in the faith. As a result, people came to speak of them not as followers of Barnabas and Paul but of Christ. Why? Because those two men modeled the Savior to people in Antioch, and multitudes were added to the faith and grew in the Lord. Later Paul would write to the church in Corinth to warn them as his beloved children (1 Cor. 4:14) and remind them of his unique relationship with them—though they may have been taught by countless others, only he had begotten them in the Gospel (v. 15). In light of this, he urged them, "Imitate me" (v. 16). Then, in the context of calling on them to live lives that glorify God in whatever they do (10:31), he said, "Imitate me, just as I also imitate Christ" (11:1).

The principle is obvious—lives that glorify God are produced, to a great degree, by following the example of others who glorify God. In essence what Paul was telling the Corinthians was "Do as you have seen me do, become a mimic, an imitator."

It's amazing how much we people can be like mockingbirds. We have the capability of imitating in our lives what we see in others. That's why setting an example of Christlikeness as Paul did is so crucial for successful discipling.

How had Paul modeled integrity? He spelled it out for the Corinthians.

> For our boasting is this: the testimony of our conscience, that we conducted ourselves in the world in simplicity and godly sincerity, not with fleshly wisdom but by the grace of God, we behaved ourselves in the world and more abundantly toward you (2 Cor. 1:12).

## A LIFE OF INTEGRITY

The apostle used two key words to describe the character of his conduct in setting an example before the Corinthians. The first of these words, *haplos*, might be translated "simplicity." It literally means "without fold." It's a word that fits well with the concept of integrity, something often lacking in our society today according to my respected friend Warren Wiersbe, whose book *The Integrity Crisis* deals with this subject in characteristically biblical fashion.

> Integrity is to personal or corporate character what health is to the body or 20/20 vision is to the eyes. A person with integrity is not divided (that's *duplicity)* or merely pretending (that's *hypocrisy*). He or she is "whole"; life is "put together," and things are working together harmoniously. People with integrity have nothing to hide and nothing to fear. Their lives are open books.[1]

That's the way the apostle Paul had lived before the Corinthians and others to whom he had ministered. His life had been an open book. Paul had no skeletons in the closet, no secrets hidden away in an upper room or a locked file cabinet. He wasn't one way in public ministry and another in private. With Paul what you saw was what you got.

## A LIFE OF SINCERITY

The other word the apostle used, "godly sincerity," was a similar Greek word meaning "transparency." In essence the apostle explained, "I've been open with you, just like God. We haven't corrupted or peddled the Word. We've had no hidden agenda with you. We've operated in the sight of God in a manner that really proves we have no need to commend or defend ourselves" (2 Cor. 2:17; 3:1).

## A BLAMELESS LIFE

Now this doesn't mean perfection. Paul wasn't perfect and wouldn't have claimed to be. Yet his life had exhibited the kind of character he talked about when he called for the elders of the church to be blameless (1 Tim. 3:2, Titus 1:6). Blamelessness isn't perfection. Peter, for example, served as an elder and identified himself as such (1 Peter 5:1–2), although Paul identified a point earlier in Peter's life when duplicity caused him to be blamed (Gal. 2:11–12). Yet the character and conduct of Peter's life, taken overall, demonstrated that blameless trait that set a Christlike example for those who would follow him.

The beginning point of our responsibility to those around us is to demonstrate Christlike character. Years ago in Sunday school we sang a little chorus that reminded us that what we are speaks so loudly the world often isn't able to hear what we say. And if we are to reach a watching world with the Good News of Jesus Christ, a godly example is absolutely essential.

The story is told of a time when missionary David Brainerd stopped among a tribe of Indians and offered to instruct them in the Christian faith. Brainerd was said to be shocked by the Indians' reply, "Why should you desire the Indians to become Christians, seeing that the Christians are so much worse than the Indians? The Christians lie, steal, and drink worse than the Indians. They first taught the Indians to be drunk, they steal to so great a degree that their rulers are obliged to hang them for it, and even that is not enough to deter others from the practice. We will not consent therefore to become Christians lest we should be as bad as they."[2]

Nothing Brainerd could say to this tribe would persuade them to reverse their decision to reject Christianity.

Few things can be as disruptive to the process of discipleship as blatant spiritual failure on the part of Christians. Sadly, this kind of trend wasn't limited to Brainerd's day. It happens in our day as well. I clearly remember an incident in which our family had sought to witness to a neighbor. We thought we were getting somewhere until he mentioned the name of an individual and asked if he attended our church. When we replied that he did, the neighbor shook his head firmly. After explaining how this man had cheated him out of a large sum of money, he went on to say, "If he's what Christianity is all about, I don't want anything to do with it."

We had hit a brick wall in our efforts to witness to this man and lead him to faith in Christ, and all because someone had failed to exhibit Christlike integrity.

## MAKING THE TIME

Yet there's more to this than just living a consistent life. When Jesus said, "I have manifested Your name to the men whom You gave Me out of the world," He implied a requirement beyond living with integrity. He was talking about an up-close-and-personal exposure to the Lord. After all, the Father had consulted with the Son on the selection of these men out of the world and given them to the Son. They were the men with whom He had spent the bulk of His time eating and sleeping, laughing and weeping, teaching and traveling. How did they come to become like Him? They were exposed to Him.

I see two essential ingredients for us to make this happen today. One is personal contact; the other, time.

Some years ago, the telephone company—there was only one back then in an effort to encourage greater use of their long-distance services ran a series of ads urging us to "reach out and touch someone." Now, it doesn't take a genius to figure out that you can't really reach out and touch someone over the telephone. You need to be there, to spend time with them.

I recall talking with Kerry, a gifted businessman who was a member of a church I pastored. Kerry had an amazing grasp of biblical truth and a winning way with people. I felt he had great potential to disciple some of the younger men in our church. But when I shared my vision with him, he shook his head in disagreement. "Don, I just don't have the time. My business takes just about all my energy—and I enjoy fishing and hunting too much to give up the rest of my time."

Even when I shared with Kerry how other men were using fishing and hunting as an opportunity to spend time with those they discipled, he still wasn't interested. He just couldn't spare the time.

I was reminded of Kerry the other day while I was producing a radio commercial to advertise a seminar Kathy and I were conducting. In the commercial, which advertised our Strengthening Family Relationships seminar, I played a song in the background entitled "The Cat's in the Cradle" sung by Harry Chapin—a ballad that ranked in the top forty pop songs in America for almost a year. In this ballad the story was told about a man who had a child who purposed to "be like you, Dad."

In this familiar ballad, the father never had time for his son—not when he was an infant in the cradle, not when he was a ten-year-old wanting to play ball, not at all during childhood.

The son went off to college and then moved away and set up a home of his own. When the roles were reversed and the father desperately wanted to spend time with the son, the young man proved he'd turned out just like his dad—he didn't have time for the relationship.

It's true in parenting and it's true in discipling, you spell *love* by T-I-M-E—time and personal contact.

I recall discussing this principle some time ago with Bill Fair, a friend who heads up a Christian camping ministry in Colorado. Bill grew up in the same church as my wife, Kathy, and he didn't hesitate to tell me that the greatest spiritual influence in his life had been the discipling of my wife's brother, Marvin.

"Your brother-in-law's been the single most important influence in my life," he told me one day as we sat in the den of my home, drinking coffee after enjoying a meal together. Now Bill had graduated from the same Bible college and seminary I had. He had been raised in a Bible-teaching church, under the ministry of a pastor who taught the Word.

"So what was it about Marvin that influenced your life to such a degree?" I asked.

"Time. That's the main thing," he quickly replied, his face reflecting a smile. "From the time I was a little fellow in Boys' Brigade, Marvin took an interest in me. I can't begin to calculate the total number of hours he invested in my life. And now when I invest time in the lives of the people I'm discipling, I'm trying to carry on Marvin's tradition. I want to have the same kind of ministry to people he had in my life."

Time and caring. Example and integrity. What important factors these are for successful discipling. I remember the story told by Howard Hendricks. Professor Hendricks was sitting in a barber shop and struck up a conversation with a boy he'd seen there before. After a while in typically bold fashion, Prof asked, "Well, who do you want to be like?" To which the young boy replied, "Mister, I ain't found nobody I want to be like." When Hendricks told the story, he was quick to note that this young man is not an exception. He went on to say that kids aren't looking for a perfect teacher—just an honest one and a growing one. Yet for so many of them the pedestals are empty.

For Peter and Andrew, James and John, the pedestal wasn't empty. They were mentored by the perfect Man, by One who assumed the responsibility of showing them the Father and who met the requirement of investing personal contact and time with them.

## FOLLOWING CHRIST'S EXAMPLE

Jesus was also the One who demonstrated the real meaning of the phrase "to manifest Your name." Jesus wasn't teaching them all the facts about various names for God in the Old Testament or having them write down copious notes about Jehovah-Jireh, Jehovah-Rapha, or El Elyon. Rather, the essence of what Jesus meant was that His life had displayed God's nature, character, and person, which is what names in the Bible were designed to show. Often in the Bible children were given names at birth that reflected personality traits that parents hoped would describe the child when he or she reached adulthood.[3] In other words, everything God the Father is, Jesus had revealed to His disciples.

Theologians define God's attributes as "those essential qualities that belong to His nature and that outwardly reveal the substance."[4] Now, space doesn't allow for us to replow the ground well covered by many theologians who have listed all the various attributes of God. However, it will help us to see a sampling of them in order to understand how Jesus reflected them to His disciples.

For example, Scripture presents God as being unchanging, "I, the Lord, do not change" (Mal. 3:6). Throughout His lifetime, Jesus demonstrated a complete consistency in word and action that went far beyond the consistency any human being has ever shown. The Master didn't feel one way about Samaritans one week and another the next. He didn't feel constrained to go to Jerusalem to face death on the cross at one point and reluctant later. His life of consistency reflected the Father's immutability.

Furthermore, God is all-knowing, or omniscient. Job spoke of God's knowing everything perfectly with faultless knowledge (Job 37:16), and Isaiah reaffirmed that the all-knowing God needs no teacher (Isa. 40:13–14).

Throughout His ministry, Jesus demonstrated His knowledge of the human heart, of circumstances, and even of the future. Nathanael was attracted to Him because Jesus knew what Nathanael was thinking when he sat under the fig tree (John 1:48). Jesus knew of rising opposition and the Pharisaic plot to kill Him, so He withdrew (Matt. 12:15). He perceived the angry thoughts of the Pharisees when He healed a man with a withered hand (Luke 6:8). Although we obviously aren't omniscient, as He is, we can and should ask God for the insight to *really* know the heart of those we disciple—to look beyond the surface.

Jesus also demonstrated God's truthfulness (Pss. 115:4–8; 119:86). Not only did Jesus affirm that He spoke truth (John 8:40), He claimed to be the truth (14:6), a claim His disciples accepted, since they had witnessed its validity.

Jesus' perfect conduct also demonstrated God's holiness, righteousness, and justice. Perhaps the clearest evidence of these attributes in Jesus' life are seen in His challenge to His worst enemies, "Which of you convicts Me of sin?" (8:46). It was a challenge to which the Pharisees were utterly unable to respond with a single charge.

Finally and most impressively, Jesus' life shared God's love, that deliberate choice by which God did what was best for us and demonstrated His own character. As the apostle John would later write, "God is love" (1 John 4:8, 16). John had clearly seen the greatest evidence of God's love incarnated in the person of the Son who came to give life (4:9–10). The veteran apostle further urged his readers, "Beloved, if God so loved us, we ought also to love one another. No one has seen God at any time. If we love one another, God abides in us, and His love has been perfected in us" (vv. 11–12). The closest to Jesus of all the disciples, John, perhaps better than any, saw how deeply Jesus cared. It was he who recorded that simple statement of compassion, "Now, Jesus loved Martha and her sister and Lazarus" (John 11:5), who told how, as the Savior stood before the tomb of the man He would restore to life, Lazarus, He wept, and how even the Jews who surrounded said, "See how He loved him!" (vv. 35–36). John and the other disciples had seen in Jesus a Man who could and did love inconsistent disciples, inhospitable Samaritans—upon whom John and his brother James wanted call down fire from heaven—lame people, blind people, lepers, publicans and sinners like Matthew, and even Judas who ultimately would betray Him.

Throughout His life Jesus demonstrated every important attribute of God. His example is a marvelous checkup for us to determine how effectively we are representing the Savior. Why not take a list of God's attributes and look at your own life and relationships, especially with those you disciple. Ask yourself honestly, "To what degree am I manifesting God's name to the people around me? Can they see God's holiness, love, and truth, His goodness, righteousness, longsuffering, mercy, and grace?"

Our initial step toward effective discipleship is to demonstrate the character of God to those around us, especially to those we disciple. Just as the Father had given Jesus the disciples so He could show them what the Father was like, so God has given us the opportunity to invest in the lives of people by first setting an example so they can see what God Himself is like.

## THE RESULT

To model the character of God before people will not go unrewarded. When Jesus manifested the Father's name to His men, He observed, "And they have kept Your Word" (17:6).

The word John uses here carries the idea "to watch, guard, or pay attention to."[5] It was often used of guarding or keeping watch over a prisoner, preserving something, or of keeping, observing, fulfilling, or paying attention to laws or teachings. It seems that is exactly what Jesus had in mind here. These men responded positively to the word He shared with them because they saw Him role-model that word in life. Later John would say, "He who says, 'I know Him,' and does not keep His commandments, is a liar, and the truth is not in him. But whoever keeps His word, truly the love of God is perfected in him" (1 John 2:4–5). There was a harmony between what Jesus said and what He lived that prompted them to respond by paying attention to the message He shared.

Furthermore, Christ's positive example gave them assurance. "Now they have known that all things which You have given me are from You" (John 17:7). To a great degree the assurance of the validity of the disciples' faith rested on both the living testimony of Jesus and the positive response of faith they gave toward His word. It's amazing what a difference a clear message and a consistent testimony can make when coupled together. In the next chapter we shall see how these disciples came to saving faith in response to the words Jesus gave them. But it was His example that laid the foundation, plowed the ground, and prepared the soil of their hearts.

Some years ago, the Communist government in China commissioned an author to write a biography of Hudson Taylor. Their purpose was to distort the facts of his life, discredit his name, and present him and the Christian faith in as bad a light as possible.

As the author conducted his research, he became increasingly impressed by Taylor's godly life and character. He continued to struggle with his conscience as he carried on his work.

Finally, at the risk of losing his life, he laid aside his project, renounced his atheism, and received Jesus as His personal Savior.

May our lives be such an example that, like the Savior, we will attract others to the character and love of the God we serve.

### ENDNOTES

1. Warren W. Wiersbe, *The Integrity Crisis* (Nashville: Thomas Nelson Publishers, 1988), 21.
2. *The Bible Illustrator* (Hiawatha, Iowa: Parsons Technology), 2996–2997.
3. J. I. Packer, Merrill C. Tenney, and William White, *The Bible Almanac* (Nashville: Thomas Nelson Publishers, 1980), 446.
4. Floyd H. Barackman, *Practical Christian Theology* (Grand Rapids: Kregel, 1992), 30.
5. Arndt and Gingrich, *A Greek-English Lexicon,* 822.

# Chapter Six

# DISCIPLESHIP STEP 2: EVANGELISM

"I gave them the Gospel" (John 17:8).

Have you noticed that most of the news we get these days is bad? I must confess to being something of a news hound. My colleague Woodrow Kroll at Back to the Bible shares my keen interest in the news. Recently over lunch he explained how he had discovered which times our local television channels cut away from the newscast for commercials. It seems he has learned how to watch almost an entire half-hour of news by switching channels at the appropriate times and missing all the commercial interruptions.

Now you may not share my fascination with the news or listen to much of today's bad news. Both the electronic and print media feed us a steady diet of robberies and rapes, murder and mayhem, natural disaster and man-made catastrophe.

The other day I came across a piece of bad news that had turned into good news—a media rarity in our day. Our local television stations and newspapers had devoted extensive coverage to the impending execution of convicted murderer Robert Williams, a death-row inmate at the state's maximum security prison. Mr. Williams was scheduled to die for two murders committed decades before.

Yet the story I heard on our local Christian radio station, KGBI, didn't focus on Mr. Williams' crimes or the efforts of his attorneys to gain a stay of execution or have his sentence commuted to life imprisonment.

Instead, the station broadcast an exclusive interview in which Robert Williams told of the ultimate reality that had changed his life. Speaking in a soft voice and without bitterness over his impending execution, Mr. Williams explained how he had come to trust in Jesus Christ as His personal Savior some time after his imprisonment. His life and values had changed drastically as he responded to the Good News of the Savior who had died to provide forgiveness even for sins Robert had committed, and who arose again to guarantee him the hope of everlasting life.

As Robert Williams put it in the March 18, 1995, edition of the *Lincoln Journal-Star,* "Now the real issue in my life is whether God wants me to die and be with Christ, which is much better, or to live and invest my life trying to reach the younger men in this prison."

Clearly the Good News of Jesus Christ has made an incredible difference in the life of Robert Williams. It has made the ultimate difference in my life as well.

## CORNERSTONE FAITH

For the first-century men who followed Jesus Christ, faith in Him became the cornerstone on which all life and ministry were based. At a point when many of Jesus' disciples began to experience adversity and some were forsaking Him, Jesus asked the Twelve, "Do you also want to go away?" To which Simon Peter, speaking for the group replied, "Lord, to whom shall we go? You have the words of eternal life. Also we have come to believe and know that You are the Christ, the Son of the living God" (John 6:67–69).

As we consider the steps Jesus took in discipling His men, as outlined in the six statements He made in His prayer to His Heavenly Father in John 17, we discover the source of the faith Peter and the other men came to express. Jesus Himself gave them the words that led to their confident faith in Him, "For I have given to them the words which You have given Me; and they have received them, and have known surely that I came forth from You; and they have believed that You sent Me" (John 17:8).

Clearly the proclamation of the message of Jesus and the salvation He offered became the focal point of the ministry of these men. The book of Acts records how Peter preached this message to thousands on the Day of Pentecost. Philip preached to multitudes in Samaria, then led an Ethiopian traveler to personal faith; and Saul of Tarsus became Paul the apostle and missionary, perhaps the single greatest human force for the spread of the Gospel in history as he traveled the world with a passion to proclaim the Good News "that Christ died for our sins according to the Scriptures, and that He was buried, and that He rose again the third day according to the Scriptures" (1 Cor. 15:3–4).

## A DIFFERENT DAY

But is the Gospel of Jesus Christ still relevant today? Is this Good News still the same life-changing force as we near the end of the twentieth century that it was in the first century? Or is Robert Williams a rare exception?

After all, according to pollster George Barna, although many people are interested in religion and even eight out of ten Americans agree that Christianity is relevant to their lives, less than half of all adults in America strongly agree that the Christian faith is relevant to the way they live today. Only 35 percent of adults in America profess to be born-again Christians, only 24 percent of those are classified as baby busters.[1] Furthermore, the proportion of adults classified as evangelical Christians has slipped from 12 percent in the early nineties to just 7 percent in Barna's latest survey in January, 1994. And while two-thirds of Americans claim to have made a personal commitment to Jesus Christ that is important in their lives, the nature of that commitment clearly has a great deal of variety.[2]

In the pluralistic world in which we live, the idea of seeking to "evangelize" or convert others to faith in Jesus Christ ranks far down the list of important church functions. A poll conducted by the Institute for Research and Social Science at the University of North Carolina in Chapel Hill found that only 32 percent of the nation's Christians considered converting people to the faith a very important activity.[3] And when a recent meeting of the National Council of Churches was presented with a document titled "An Invitation to Evangelism" at its November, 1993, meeting in Baltimore—a document which contained the words "through the Gospel we are set free from sin . . . born from above by the Spirit as we put our faith in the crucified and risen Lord"—there was a great deal of controversy and mixed reaction.[4]

However, while the importance of evangelism may be debated in many circles today, it was clearly a priority to Jesus Christ. Speaking in His home synagogue in Nazareth during the early days in His ministry, He referenced the prophet Isaiah to explain that His Father had sent Him "to preach the Gospel" to the poor. Then, following His resurrection, He urged His disciples to go into all the world "and preach the Gospel to every creature" (Matt. 28:19).

The phrase "preach the Gospel" appears eleven times in the New Testament, nine from the prolific pen of Paul the apostle. Three times in Romans he spoke of his passion to preach the Gospel in Rome and in places where Christ had not been named (1:15; 10:15; 15:20; and also 2 Cor. 10:16). His other references to the primary task of his life can be found in his letters to the Corinthians, where he details his personal commitment to the call to preach the Gospel, a call he referred to in Acts 16:10.

Paul's first and foremost concern was to communicate a clear Gospel message, the message he later summarized in his statements about the death and resurrection of Christ in First Corinthians 15:3–4. He told the Corinthians, "For Christ did not send me to baptize, but to preach the gospel; not with wisdom of words, lest the cross of Christ should be made of no effect" (1 Cor. 1:17). Paul wasn't trying to present a sophisticated message—in fact the Greek word translated wisdom is the word *sophos,* from which we get our English term "sophisticated," and the term for "word," *logos,* is the origin of our word "logic." Paul's interest was not in sophisticated logic but in a clear presentation of the message he had been given.

I've worked in radio for many years and even taught radio communication for a few years in college. One of the things I've learned is that there are many sophisticated ways to process the sounds of music and voice that are transmitted over

AM and FM radio outlets. Typically these are designed to help the signal "punch through" more effectively on the AM band, or have more clarity and clout on FM.

Usually an extensive amount of sound processing is used for almost every music format except one—classical. The reason is simple. Classical purists want to hear the music as close to the way it was originally recorded as possible. They aren't interested in having the sound amplified, compressed, or expanded. They don't care to have a heavier bass or crisper high-frequency sounds. They want Mozart, Bach, and Vivaldi the way it was played in the first place.

That's the kind of concern Paul had for presenting a clear message, and it's a concern based on the origin of the message noted by Jesus in John 17:8.

### ORIGIN OF THE MESSAGE

In explaining how He evangelized His men, the Master pointed out, "I have given them the words You gave Me." For Jesus, who was the ultimate Word, the *logos* of God, there was a twofold concern in life—to manifest His Father's name (demonstrate the character) to His disciples and at the same time to communicate the words—*rhemata*, or utterances—that would make known to them exactly what the Father intended for them to know.

The apostle John, who recorded Jesus' prayer, began his gospel by identifying Jesus as the Word, the ultimate representation of God the Father. After establishing that He, the Word, was God (1:3), John pointed out how "the Word became flesh and dwelt among us, and we beheld His glory, the glory as of the only begotten of the Father, full of grace and truth" (v. 14). Later he would acknowledge the ultimate purpose of his gospel, "These are written that you may believe that Jesus is the Christ, the Son of God, and that believing you may have life in His name" (20:31).

This Word on whom John focuses our attention was the ultimate Source of both life and light (1:4). His coming into the world made God's light available to every person (v. 9). Despite the reality of wholesale rejection and ignorance (vv. 10–11), He offered a new life and relationship with God to all those who would receive Him by believing on His name (v. 12). Everyone who responds by trusting Him experiences the new birth—a birth achieved not by physical or national lineage, personal effort, or the endeavors of others, but accomplished by God Himself (v. 13).

As Jesus modeled the reality of the Father before mankind and especially before His men, He incorporated two important techniques for evangelism—mass and one-to-one—and He used both in the context of day to day events. For Jesus, evangelism was as natural a part of life as eating, sleeping, and breathing. John's record of His conversations with Nicodemus and with the woman at Jacob's well in Samaria provide us with examples of personal evangelism, and His message about the Bread of Life after feeding the five thousand (John 6) and His discourse on the Light of the World (John 8) provide examples of mass-evangelistic preaching. In every such instance, it is clear to see that Jesus didn't invent a message. Instead the message He delivered was the same one He had received from His Father. It's the message to which Peter and the other disciples responded, the message that changed their lives.

Early in his ministry the apostle Paul recognized how he had been entrusted with a message of divine origin. Six times he used the phrase "the Gospel of God" to describe his message. In Romans 1:1 he introduced himself as "called to be an apostle, separated to the gospel of God." Recognizing that his own life was inextricably bound up in the spread of that Good News message, he later explained the focus of his ministry of the Gospel of God to Gentiles (15:16), a ministry designed to allow people from the nations of the world to be made acceptable to God through the work of the Spirit. In defending his ministry in 2 Corinthians 11:12, Paul explained how he preached the Gospel of God freely, without charge. Writing to the newly established church in Thessalonica, Paul described how the ministry of God's Gospel was to be conducted boldly (1 Thess. 2:2), compassionately (v. 8), and persistently (v. 9). Nor did shameful treatment or adversity stop Paul from delivering God's message (v. 2). An intense love for people and a willingness to invest in their lives motivated him to impart the Gospel (v. 8). Furthermore, he was willing to work tirelessly, night and day, in order to be able to preach the Gospel in its freedom (v. 9).

Many times today we lack clarity in communicating the gospel message. In his excellent collection of material to illustrate the Gospel, Michael Green includes a dialog which illustrates how many well-meaning Christians use terms that the nonbeliever doesn't use or uses in a different way.[5] In this dialog an evangelist has stopped to witness to the clerk in a rural store. "Are you a member of the Christian family?" he asks.

"No," the clerk replies, "they live two miles down the road in the white house on the left."

"Let me try again," the evangelist continues. "Are you lost?"

"Nope," the store clerk replies, "I've lived in this town over thirty years now. I know right where I am."

So the evangelist tries again. "Let me put it this way—Are you ready for the Judgment Day?"

"When will it be?"

"Could be today, or it could be tomorrow," the evangelist replied with a note of enthusiasm.

To which the store clerk responded, "Well, when you know exactly which one, be sure to let me know. My wife will probably want to go on both days."

It's so easy for us to get our own code words wrapped up in the spread of the Gospel and obscure the fact that, for Jesus, the central issue was trust. Over and over again the Master used the word "believe" to demonstrate what a person does to respond to the Gospel. In John 1:12, John clarified the concept beautifully by using an alternative word, "receive." First he contrasted receiving with rejection, explaining how Jesus' own people had not received Him. Then John invited anyone who will to receive Him, to "welcome Him into your life." Then he explains how it works. "It's an act of personal trust, of placing your faith in Jesus Christ and who He is and what He did."

## NEAR IDENTICAL STATEMENTS

I'm suggesting that when Jesus said to His disciples, "I have given them Your words," He was talking about evangelism. Now, there are two statements in Jesus' prayer in John 17 which appear at first glance to be identical. In verse 8, He says, "I have given them the words You gave Me." Then a few moments later, He explains, "I have given them Your word . . ." (v. 14).

A close examination of these almost-identical phrases shows two clear-cut differences. First, the word translated "words" in verse 8 is *rhēmata,* while another word, *logos,* is used in verse 14. While both words find their origin in the root word *legō,* "to speak," *rhemata* is generally used to signify "a saying, a specific statement, or what is definitely stated as in an announcement, a military order, or a statement."[6] *Logos,* on the other hand, is a word with a wide range of meanings. In its secular use it often referred to a ground or plea—in fact Plato used it to describe what he called "the life-force bringing the world to birth," and Aristotle saw it as "the generative, philosophical principle existing in all organisms, causing them to reach their destiny."[7] According to Nigel Turner, however, *logos* in Scripture speaks of both Christ the eternal Word and the sacred written message from God.

While it is impossible to be dogmatic by saying that in every instance in Scripture *rhēma* speaks of the gospel message and *logos* the "whole counsel of God," this seems to be the way Jesus used the two terms in this prayer. I believe this difference can be seen from the second distinction between the two statements—the difference in response. Their response when Jesus gave them the *rhēmata* (v. 8) was "They have received them and have known surely that I came forth from You, and they have believed that You sent Me." In simple language this sounds like saving faith and assurance.

Then in verse 14 when He says, "I have given them your *logon,*" He explained that this would lead to an increasing alienation from the world, as they were sanctified through the Word which is truth (v. 14–17). Thus it appears to me that Jesus is making these two statements to look at two different aspects of the process of discipleship, justification (saving faith) and sanctification (Christian growth).

Clearly the common denominator for these two processes is the Word of God. As the apostle Paul told the Romans, "Faith comes by hearing, and hearing by the Word of God" (Rom. 10:13). Later the apostle reminded Timothy that all Scripture is profitable for doctrine, reproof, correction, and instruction in right living, and that in light of these truths the young man Paul mentored was to "preach the Word" (2 Tim. 3:16–4:2).

In short, it seems to me that verse 8 refers to the process

we commonly call evangelism, while verse 14 looks at edifi-
cation, or teaching the body of truth. This may have been
what Paul had in mind in Acts 20:27 when he reminded the
Ephesian elders, "I have not shunned to declare to you the
whole counsel of God." Since he said in the preceding verse
he was free of the blood of all men, Paul may have had both
processes in mind.

Just the mention of the word "evangelism" can be enough
to create negative thoughts in the minds of many Christians,
thoughts ranging from "guilt trip" conversions to "scalp
hunting" confrontations. When I was in Bible college, I knew
of individuals who drove through poverty-stricken neighborhoods, in the States and in some foreign countries, en-
gaging in what they referred to as "gospel bombing." Perhaps
they really did think that throwing tightly wrapped bundles
of gospel tracts—not well-printed for the most part—out
the window of their car at poor children was an effective
way to communicate the love and grace of Jesus Christ, but
it wasn't.

## MISCONCEPTIONS OF EVANGELISM

Think with me for a minute about some of the evangelism misconceptions we have today. Perhaps the first and
most obvious that comes to mind is that evangelism is
something done by either evangelists or preachers. Frankly,
I've known both evangelists and preachers who have done
an extremely effective job of evangelism. As I'm writing this
chapter, the best-known evangelist in our generation, Billy
Graham, is conducting a crusade in San Juan, Puerto Rico.
Mr. Graham's staff estimates that eight million people will
attend satellite crusades, which will be held in 185 countries and territories during the following weeks. One billion
people are expected to view the video crusades and prime
time broadcasts in a total of 117 countries, including the
United States.

Clearly not everyone can share the Gospel using satellite
technology, massive stadiums, or the kind of methods Mr.
Graham employs. That's just one form of evangelism.

Let me use three men I've come to know rather well to
illustrate different kinds of evangelism. Larry, a classmate
of mine from seminary, has the gift of evangelism. Since our

seminary days, he has been involved in conducting evangelistic crusades in churches, stadiums, and other settings in the United States and other countries. Larry is committed to taking specific passages of Scripture and expounding them to clearly present the Gospel of the grace of God.

Gus was a member of a church I pastored in central Texas. When we invited Larry to come to our city to conduct a crusade, Gus and his wife ran a "mom and pop" hardware store. Gus was basically a shy individual. Early in my pastoral ministry he asked me not to call on him to pray or speak in public. "I just get too emotional when I'm called on that way. I may freeze up or even start weeping."

Although he never spoke publicly or preached an evangelistic sermon, Gus in his own way was just as evangelism-minded as Larry. Few people traded with Gus at his store without hearing of the Savior he loved. He had a heart for people and an ability to speak one-on-one. Like Larry, Gus was an evangelist.

Hal, another friend, employed some of the same strategies both Larry and Gus used. At times, both as a pastor and a missionary, he would preach an evangelistic sermon. However, Hal's favorite approach was to take a group of unsaved individuals—perhaps a family or two—and engage in a series of evangelistic Bible studies. Numerous individuals in the United States and Mexico can point to Hal as their spiritual father because of his efforts in what he likes to call "discipleship evangelism."

These men illustrate three different styles of evangelism. None is the only "right way," and none is the "wrong way."

A second common evangelism misconception is "I don't need to do it or shouldn't do it because I don't have the gift." There are many things in Scripture that *some* Christians are gifted for, but *all* Christians are to do. For example, giving is clearly identified as a spiritual gift (Rom. 12:8), yet the same apostle who described this gift also urged every believer to participate in "first day of the week" giving (1 Cor. 16:2). In the same Romans passage Paul included the gift of showing mercy, yet James suggested that wise Christians will all be controlled by mercy and good fruits (James 3:17). So it's wrong for me to conclude that just because I don't have the spiritual gift of evangelism, I don't need to be sharing the Gospel.

A third misconception is "I don't want to get involved in evangelism. Too many people have misused the process." Sure, there are those who have been "ambushed for Jesus," subjected to what Joe Aldrich calls "evangelical mugging."[8] However, in all my years of ministry I can just about count on the fingers of one hand all the people I've known who demonstrated an overabundance of boldness or a "grab them by the lapels, shake them, and ask them, 'heaven or hell, which for you?'" mentality. Far more people seem to suffer from what might be described as evangelistic lockjaw. Or to put it another way, when they have the opportunity to share the Gospel, they're like an arctic river—frozen over at the mouth.

Yet another misconception—and I'm including just a few of many involving this important topic—is "My gift is something else, not evangelism. Since I major in other responsibilities such as teaching the Word, showing mercy, or administrative leading, God doesn't expect me to be involved in evangelism."

My friend Larry came up with what I believe is the best response to this misconception I've ever heard. As he put it one night on my radio call-in program, *Life Perspectives*, "Sharing the Good News of His Son with lost people is close to God's heart. I think it's important that we be involved in doing anything that's close to the heart of God, and what can you find closer to the heart of God than sharing the Gospel with lost people and inviting them to the Savior?"

Let's consider a final misconception: "I want to be a living witness, not a verbal one."

The fact is, God expects us to be both. Christlikeness includes both living and communicating the Good News. As we see throughout John's gospel, Jesus was both the living "*logos*" and the One who spoke the words of God to people. Not only did He manifest the Father's name to His men, He also gave them the words the Father had given Him.

## CHRIST'S EXAMPLE OF EVANGELISM

Jesus also provided the men He called with the opportunity to see Him present the Good News to people, both individually and in groups. John the evangelist presents several such instances in his gospel that show how the process works.

The first instance involved an evening encounter with a man named Nicodemus, one of the religious leaders in Israel (John 3). Nicodemus was one of the Sanhedrin, a respected member of the party of the Pharisees, a man who knew the Old Testament well. Perhaps convinced by the miracles Jesus had performed, he recognized the Nazarene as a rabbi and acknowledged that God was with Him.

Jesus replied without mincing words, flattering, or beating around the bush. He came straight to the point. "Unless one is born again, he cannot see the kingdom of God" (v. 3).

How amazing! Nicodemus hadn't even voiced the question in his heart, and already Jesus had given him the answer. Assuming they were present, John and the other disciples must have been taken aback with the Lord's straightforward approach.[9] Then Nicodemus replied with a question, "How can a man be born when he is old?" He didn't fully grasp the word picture the Savior had used to show him that he—Nicodemus—needed to change his mind about the way to be right with God. Good works or improving one's efforts to please God would never do. What was required was a totally new life—the result of new birth!

In His reply Jesus demonstrated an important principle for us to remember as we witness—we need to be aware of the frame of reference and needs of people we encounter. While we don't have the omniscience of Jesus, we do have the indwelling Spirit who can direct us, and the sword of the Spirit—the written Word—at our disposal.

When Nicodemus admitted he didn't understand what Jesus what getting at, the Master clarified with yet another word picture to show that there are two different realities, the natural or visible reality and the spiritual. Every human is born of the flesh; some meet God's requirement and are born of the Spirit. Then He used another word picture, the wind, which cannot be visibly observed except for its results. Jesus seemed to be saying, "It's humanly impossible to look at a person and say, 'I know for sure this person has been born again.' However, there are certain evidences or results, just as with the wind, that demonstrate the reality of the Spirit's presence in a person's life."

As the disciples listened, perhaps with mouths agape, Nicodemus, the religious expert, asked, "How can these things be?" To which Jesus replied, "Are you the teacher of

Israel, and do not know these things? Most assuredly, I say to you, We speak what We know and testify what We have seen, and you do not receive Our witness" (vv. 10–11).

At this point the Lord zeroed in on the real lesson of saving faith, and He did so by dipping into the wealth of Old Testament Scripture with which Nicodemus was so familiar. He brought up the time when Israel wandered in the wilderness, an incident occurred in which venomous snakes brought painful death to many Israelites. Following God's instructions, Moses made a snake of bronze, set it on a pole, and invited anyone who had been bitten to look at the bronze snake and be healed (Num. 21). Certainly Nicodemus couldn't miss the point, for Jesus went on to say that "as Moses lifted up the serpent in the wilderness, even so must the Son of Man be lifted up, that whoever believes in Him should not perish but have eternal life" (John 3:14–15).

We cannot help marveling at the clarity with which Jesus communicated the message to this religious leader. Nicodemus certainly understood the point of Old Testament story. No amount of good works could save any of the Israelites who had been bitten by the serpent. But all they had to do was look in faith at the symbol God had told them to lift up on a pole—a substitute snake. In the same way, Jesus explained, the Son of Man—the term was one of the familiar words of the Old Testament to describe the Messiah, the One sent by God to be Israel's Redeemer—would be lifted up to provide life to those who believed in Him. Little wonder that, after Jesus has been lifted up on a cross outside Jerusalem, Nicodemus joined Joseph of Arimathea in the Master's burial and became identified with His followers (John 19:39).

The clarity of Jesus' communication of the gospel message was supported by compassion, as He went on to share with Nicodemus what has become the best-loved verse in the entire Bible, a verse used to lead countless thousands to faith in the Savior, "For God so loved the world that He gave His only begotten Son, that whoever believes in Him should not perish but have everlasting life" (John 3:16).

What an amazing statement of compassion! God gave His Son. What an incredible invitation! Whoever believes in Him. What an amazing promise! The one who trusts Him will not perish, but be given everlasting life.

Note that Jesus didn't push Nicodemus for an immediate decision. He simply did what He would later explain to His disciples in the parables of the soils. He sowed the seed and left the results to His Father, who would apply the Word by His Spirit. In similar fashion, preaching the Gospel is like sowing the seed of the Word. Our responsibility is not to force people to trust Christ. Our mission is *witness*, to give our own testimony based on God's Word and our experience of the Living Word, the Savior. As someone so aptly said, it's like one beggar telling another beggar where to find food.

However, the Master made sure that the issues of faith or rejection and their results were crystal clear. To do so, He used a fourth word picture, the contrast between light and darkness (vv. 19–21). Those who continue to practice evil refuse to come to the light, but those who trust Him have come to live in the light. Jesus used no emotional gimmicks or mental tricks, nor did He employ any sales techniques. He just brought the key issues—sin, righteousness, and judgment—into the light. "I am the way, the truth and the life. No one comes to the Father except through Me" (14:6).

## WITNESS TO AN OUTCAST

In the following chapter John presented a remarkable contrast as Jesus and His men headed into territory no self-respecting Jew would even travel through—Samaria. They stopped at a familiar well, one which had belonged to the patriarch Jacob, and Jesus' disciples headed into town, leaving Him alone.

The woman who came to that well at noonday afforded Jesus an excellent opportunity to utilize additional principles of evangelism in a different setting—what elements of the message could be adapted and which needed to be maintained. Nicodemus was a Jewish man, educated and wealthy, from the upper echelon of society. This woman, however, had questionable morals, was a member of a mixed race of people, and was probably an outcast even from her own people, since she came to the well alone and at noon.

However, Jesus seized the opportunity, and as He must have explained to His disciples later in great detail, He initiated the conversation by asking the woman for a drink. One of Jesus' most effective evangelistic techniques can be see here, as well as in His contact with Zacchaeus (Luke 19:1–10). In both instances Jesus allowed the unsaved individual to do something for Him in the physical realm before inviting them to trust Him in the spiritual realm.

Jesus adapted to both the setting at the well and the woman herself. She was intrigued and surprised that He, a Jewish man, would ask water from a Samaritan woman (v. 9).

Without hesitation, Jesus honed in on the most important issue He wanted to discuss with this woman which was the gift of God, and who it is who says to you, 'Give Me a drink'" (v. 10). Without hesitation, He explained that she only needed to ask of Him to receive the gift of living water (vv. 10, 14).

However, the woman totally missed the point. Like Nicodemus and so many of our day, she could only see things in terms of the immediate and the physical. In essence, her reply reflected the thought, *What an opportunity! If I could just get a source of water that would keep me from having to come out to this well in the heat of the day. . . .*

As He explained His ability to meet her need, Jesus identified the woman's deepest need, and He did so with the same skill Nathan demonstrated when he confronted David with his sin. "Go, call your husband, and come here," He urged (v. 16). When she replied, seemingly without hesitation or thought, "I have no husband," Jesus immediately pinpointed this most clear-cut evidence of her spiritual need. "You have had five husbands, and the one whom you now have is not your husband" (v. 18).

This revelation brought about from her an immediate effort to change the subject: "What is the correct place for worship?" she asked. Countless thousands, confronted by the Gospel since that day, have taken the Samaritan woman's approach and changed the focus of the conversation. Yet Jesus refused to be swayed from the critical issue of faith in Him which leads to worship in spirit and truth. Instead He brought her back to the question, How can you be right with God?

That question prompted her to acknowledge that the ultimate answer rested in the promised Messiah. So Jesus drove home the point of the conversation with the words,

"I who speak to you am He" (v. 26). At this point the disciples arrived and were shocked to find Him talking with this woman.

Later, when the disciples urged Him to eat, He said, "I have food to eat of which you do not know. . . . My food is to do the will of Him who sent Me, and to finish His work." Then Jesus used a word picture with His disciples to portray the urgency of spreading the Gospel. "Look at the fields," perhaps as He gestured toward the surrounding landscape. "You would say there are four months until harvest, but I say to you, lift up your eyes and look on the fields, for they are white already to harvest." Using the agricultural motif, Jesus explained that "both he that soweth and he that reapeth may rejoice together."

Almost immediately the woman must have returned with people from the Samaritan city who had come to trust in Him because of the testimony of the woman who had become an evangelist herself. Then many more believed as He taught in their village for the next two days (vv. 39–42).

## DELIVERING THE MESSAGE

The concept of evangelizing is built on the foundation of two crucial words—*euaḡgelízomai* and *kērussō*. Both of these grow out of Old Testament concepts of proclaiming good news about God's powerful acts and ultimate victorious rule (Pss. 40:10; 68:11). The herald was to proclaim God's mighty deeds among the people of Israel. The Greeks used *euaḡgelízomai* for proclaiming the news of victory in battle or death or the capture of an enemy.[10] John the Baptist proclaimed the Good News of the coming of Messiah (Luke 3:18), and Jesus Himself preached the Gospel (Matt. 11:5; Luke 4:18; 7:22). *Euaḡgelízo* seems to focus more on the content of the message, while *kērussō* looks at the activity of proclaiming that message.

The apostle Paul brings the two terms together in Romans 10:15, a verse that clearly delineates how the process of evangelism works. In verse 13 the apostle pointed out that faith comes by hearing the Word of God. The following verse shows the need for someone to serve as a herald and spread "the news" of Jesus' provision for salvation. Then in verse 15, the apostle tied the two terms together utilizing a quote from Isaiah 52:7: "How shall they preach [*kērussō*, or herald the message] unless they are sent? As it is written, 'How beautiful are the feet of those who preach the gospel of peace, who bring glad tidings of good things!' [to understand or spread the Good News]."

One danger we face in trying to understand these terms is reading our modern-day conceptions about preachers and evangelists back into them. While *kērussō* can speak of what we consider preaching today, it seems to be a broader term than that. One source notes that "even if we disregard the other terms and restrict ourselves to 'preach' in translation of *kērussō*, the term is not a strict equivalent of what the New Testament means. [It] does not mean the delivery of a learned and edifying oratory or discourse in well-chosen words and a pleasant voice. It is the declaration of an event. It's true sense is to proclaim."[11]

For Paul, preaching the Gospel was a major life focus as he functioned as a herald to get the message out. The phrase "preach the Gospel" can be found eleven times in the New Testament. Jesus used it early in His ministry, quoting from Isaiah 61 of his mission (Luke 4:18). He mandated that His followers go into all the world and preach the Gospel to everyone (Mark 16:15.) Luke, in his account of Paul's career, underscores the apostle's sense of calling to preach the Gospel (Acts 16:10). Paul himself expressed a strong commitment to preach the Gospel in Rome (Rom. 1:15) and anywhere the Gospel had not been preached (15:20), since even the feet of those who preached the Gospel were considered beautiful (10:15). Writing to the Corinthians, the apostle underscored his own calling to preach the Gospel apart from sophisticated logic (1 Cor. 1:17). Furthermore, while the Lord had appointed some to preach the Gospel as a vocation (9:14), for Paul it was more—it was a compulsion (v. 16), and an activity to be done without any abuse of finances or authority (v. 18).

Like the task of modern news anchors, our mission is to "deliver the news" accurately. In our case the news is Jesus' death and resurrection and the salvation He offers to those who place their trust in Him. This can be done in sermon form, one-to-one conversations, or small-group discussions. It can take place on an airplane, over a kitchen table, or on a park bench. The point is, Jesus preached the Gospel with His men, and He expects each of us to deliver the Good News today.

## RESPONDING TO THE MESSAGE

In His prayer, Jesus explained how He had delivered the words that originated in the Father to His men and prompted a response. "They have received them, and have known surely that I came forth from You; and they have believed that You sent Me" (John 17:8).

The tense of the verb indicates an action that took place at a point of time. In other words, there was a point when each of these disciples recognized his own need for a Savior, came to understand that Jesus had come from God to provide their salvation, and placed trust in Him.

Ironically, the New Testament does not give us with absolute certainty the point at which each of these men trusted Christ. In fact there is some disagreement as to when Peter, James, John, and some of the other disciples actually came to saving faith.

Perhaps there is a great lesson for us in that since we are often keenly interested in making sure we know the exact moment when a person has trusted Christ. Certainly pinpointing when one has trusted Christ can be helpful in providing an individual with assurance. However, the statement Jesus made in John 17:8 simply indicates that by the time when He was praying, these men had come to an assurance of faith. My ministry experience has led me to the conviction that it is much more important that a person have the assurance at present that they have actually trusted Christ, than that they are able to pinpoint the precise time when they exercised saving faith.

The important issue of salvation is to have the assurance that we have indeed trusted Christ. Knowing a date can be helpful, but it's not the primary issue. When we speak of becoming a Christian, the issue is trusting Christ for salvation. When we speak of discipleship, the issue is following Christ and learning from Him. Just as with physical birth, becoming a Christian occurs at a point in time. Jesus used the aorist tense in Greek to indicate that they had believed (v. 8) and were members of the household of faith. Perhaps prior to this time they became disciples and began learning from Him.

This brings up another question, one we raised earlier. Can a person be a disciple without becoming a Christian? Certainly the evidence in John 6 indicates that many disciples who heard Jesus' teaching, especially about His being the Bread of Life, quit following Him. Furthermore, in John 2 there were many who committed themselves to Jesus—the word used is *pisteuō* (trusting). Yet Jesus did not commit Himself—*pisteuō*, the same word—to them (vv. 23–24). He knew their hearts; He recognized that what may have seemed like genuine faith to outside observers wasn't real faith at all. Later, he would tell the group who followed Him and were identified as His disciples that "there are some of you who do not believe" (6:60, 64).

I am convinced that there are times when the process of discipleship begins prior to conversion. I saw this happen in the life of a husky, dark-haired man named Ron, a former college football player, who along with his wife became friends with my wife and me. Even though Ron wasn't interested in spiritual issues, he and I began fishing together. We discussed the Gospel a number of times, and his life and values began to reflect a growing interest in the things of Christ.

After sharing the Gospel with Ron, I invited him to study God's Word, which he began doing for himself. At this point in his life, I think it would have been accurate to refer to Ron as a disciple. However, he clearly was not yet a Christian.

I had encouraged Ron to place his faith in the Savior, and I told him that when he reached that decision, I'd like to be one of the first to know. Then one evening as we were sitting down to dinner, the doorbell rang. When I opened the door, there stood Ron—a smile as big the state of Texas across his face. I immediately realized what had happened, and within moments Ron told me. "Don, I did what you said. I trusted Christ." Now Ron had become a Christian. Of course, his development as a disciple accelerated significantly as, led by the indwelling Spirit, he began to learn and master new truths.

What had happened? Ron had finally responded to the Good News that I and others had shared with him. The seed of the Word had taken root and born fruit.

That is the essence of evangelism, and it's one of the most exciting and important elements in the process of discipleship.

## ENDNOTES

1. George Barna, *Virtual America* (Ventura, Calif.: Regal Books, 1994), 97, 107.
2. Ibid., 109–10.
3. *Christian Century*, 15–22 June 1994, 601.
4. *Christianity Today*, 7 February 1994, 19.
5. Michael P. Green, ed., *Illustrations for Biblical Preaching* (Grand Rapids: Baker, 1982), 123–24.
6. Kittel, *Theological Dictionary*, vol. 4, 75.
7. Nigel Turner, *Christian Words* (London: T & T Clark Limited, 1981), 494–95.
8. Joseph C. Aldrich, *Life-Style Evangelism* (Portland, Oreg.: Multnomah Press, 1981), 19.
9. Since Jesus and the disciples traveled together and Nicodemus came to where Jesus was, John's detailed account of their conversation would seem to affirm that the disciples were present during this interview.
10. Kittel, *Theological Dictionary*, vol. 2, 710.
11. Ibid., vol. 3, 703.

Chapter Seven

# DISCIPLESHIP STEP 3: INTERCESSION

"I pray for them" (John 17:9).

Many years ago, during a difficult time in my ministry, a friend told me, "Don, I'm praying for you and for your ministry. In fact, I'm committed to praying for your ministry every day." Knowing the commitment of this individual to the Lord and to prayer, I'm confident that I continue to benefit from my friend's ministry of intercession.

Some time ago a dear lady, a widow who has suffered a great deal of pain and affliction, said to me, "Don, I've prayed for your ministry daily over the last five years. And I plan to keep praying for you as long as God leaves me here."

Do you have people who pray for you? Few things in life are as encouraging as being told by someone whose prayer life you respect that they are praying for you.

Someone has well said, "You can do more than pray, but you cannot do more until you have first prayed." When we are with people, we can encourage them. Sometimes we can "reach out and touch them" by telephone. But space and time never limit the opportunity we have to intercede for others before the throne of Grace.

## A DOOR TO GOD

Some years ago a Sunday school teacher asked a group of children, "What is meant by intercession?" One of the children replied, "Speaking a word to God for us, sir."

That's the essence of prayer and how it works. According to Samuel Zwemer, "True prayer is God the Holy Spirit talking to God the Father in the name of God the Son, and the believer's heart is the prayer-room."[1]

The most meaningful example of intercession is the prayer ministry of Jesus. Some time ago I spent several days with my parents to celebrate their fiftieth wedding anniversary. Both of them have walked with the Lord since early in my life and have had a profound spiritual impact on me. So I paid close attention when Mother told me she'd discovered a song that had become her all-time favorite. We had never heard the song before, but once we secured a tape of it, Kathy and I decided we wanted to sing it, and we've used it several times since then. The song that has been so special to my mother is entitled "And He's Ever Interceding," and it's based on Hebrews 7:25: "Therefore He is also able to save to the uttermost those who come to God through Him, since He always lives to make intercession for them."

Picture the disciples listening to the Lord Jesus lift His voice in prayer to His heavenly Father and imagine the pain and anxiety of their impending separation from Him. Their hearts must have been lifted immeasurably when they heard His words, "I pray for them. I do not pray for the world but for those whom You have given Me, for they are Yours. And all Mine are Yours, and Yours are Mine, and I am glorified in them" (John 17:9–10).

What a remarkable statement by Jesus: "I pray for them."

Earlier that same evening they had been reminded—Peter especially—of the Lord's commitment to intercede with His heavenly Father on their behalf. Ironically they had been arguing over which of them would be recognized as greatest in the kingdom (Luke 22:44). They were also distraught because they had learned that one of them would betray Jesus (vv. 22–23). After reminding them of the importance of developing a servant's heart, the Lord assured them that since they had been with Him during the trials He had suffered (v. 28), they would also participate in His coming kingdom.

Then, just as their hearts must have begun to feel a touch of relief, the Lord turned to Simon Peter and said, "Simon, Simon! Indeed, Satan has asked for you, that he may sift you as wheat." Now these men had been raised in an agricultural setting—they all understood the process of sifting. They couldn't have missed the point of Jesus' vivid word picture.

Then the Lord went on to say, "But I have prayed for you, that your faith should not fail." In essence what Jesus was saying is, "Peter, your spiritual perseverance—your very future in serving Me—rests on My praying for you. And I'm confident, Peter, that My prayer will be answered. So when you are turned back, I want you to strengthen your brethren."

Unfortunately, what happened next wasn't uncommon for Peter and the other disciples. Peter in essence replied, "Lord, no problem—I'm ready to go to prison with You, or to die with You, whatever." And Mark adds the editorial comment, "Likewise they all said." It wasn't until later that Peter would remember the Lord's warning about his threefold denial (v. 34).

I wonder if we really appreciate the impact of the ministry of intercession that others carry on for us. Recently our church has begun publishing a prayer update, allowing the entire church family to focus on specific, meaningful prayer requests for our pastoral staff, our missionaries, and our upcoming ministry events and activities.

Since intercessory prayer is such an integral part of Jesus' ministry in heaven today, since it occupied such a priority place in His life on earth, and since prayer is a major focus throughout Scripture, it makes sense to focus on prayer as an important aspect in the process of discipling. Certainly Jesus made it a key element in discipling His men—and He wasn't hesitant to let them know it. Usually when we think of discipling, we think of challenging people to commitment, teaching them biblical truths, holding them accountable, or motivating them to disciple others. Yet prayer is the unseen element that fuels the process of discipleship.

Unfortunately, prayer is an often-overlooked element in spiritual vitality today. Sometimes we approach it like the man who said, "I'm sorry, all I can do for you is pray—I'll try to do better next time." Or we view prayer as a relatively harmless, typically meaningless ritual on the order of "Now I lay me down to sleep, I pray the Lord my soul to keep." Or as a little sign in a principal's office stated, "In the event of nuclear attack, fire, or earthquake, the ban on prayer will be temporarily lifted."

## A LINE OF COMMUNICATION

One of the best descriptions of prayer comes from Warren Wiersbe, who has labeled it "the thermometer of our spiritual lives."[2] By means of prayer we communicate directly and instantaneously with the throne of grace, the very presence of God in heaven. It's our line of communication, our network connecting us and others with the Lord Himself.

Without question, communication is absolutely essential, especially in warfare or the athletic arena. Many professional and college football games have been lost because communication broke down between a team and its quarterback or coach. Many a military victory has been won—or lost—as a result of communication between commanding officers and front line troops.

Prayer is just that. It's one side of the link in the essential two-way communication between the Lord's followers—His frontline troops—and divine headquarters in heaven. Think about it. In 54 B.C. it took twenty-nine days to get a letter from the imperial capital of Rome to Julius Caesar in Britain. Today we can communicate by global satellite in just over a second to any location on earth. We can send a signal from the earth to the moon in 2.6 seconds. But prayer is even quicker, it's instantaneous.[3]

Individuals from all walks of life have recognized the importance of prayer. Abraham Lincoln is often quoted as saying, "I have been driven many times to my knees by the overwhelming conviction that I had nowhere else to go. My own wisdom, and that of all about me seemed insufficient for the day."[4] Respected confederate general Stonewall Jackson was such a man of prayer that he never raised a glass of water to his lips, sealed a letter, or changed the wording of the classes he taught at the military academy without lifting a prayer to God.[5] William Carey was once rebuked for spending so much time in prayer that he neglected his business. To which he replied, "Prayer is my real business, cobbling shoes is just a sideline to help me pay expenses."[6] And a young student once asked Charles H. Spurgeon, "What is the secret of your power? What work will I have to do to get the power you have?" To which Mr. Spurgeon quickly answered, "Knee work, young man! Knee work!" Spurgeon is also quoted as saying, "I would rather teach one man to pray than ten men to preach."[7] And Andrew Murray said, "The man who mobilizes the Christian church to pray will make the greatest contribution to world evangelization in history."[8]

There's a familiar quote from Samuel Chadwick: "The one concern of the Devil is to keep Christians from praying. He fears nothing from prayerless studies, prayerless work, or prayerless religion. He laughs at our toil, mocks at our wisdom, but he trembles when we pray."[9]

So why do we struggle so greatly with prayer? Perhaps we don't really understand how it works. As Philips Brooks said, "Prayer is not the conquering of God's reluctance, but the taking hold of God's willingness."[10] It's not changing God's mind about what to do, but adjusting ourselves to what is His will.

In addition, we often feel we're just too busy to pray. A former United States Senate chaplain, Peter Marshall, once prayed publicly, "Forgive us for thinking that prayer is a waste of time and help us to see that without prayer our work is a waste of time."[11]

## PRAYER IN SCRIPTURE

As a nation, Israel was born out of the prayer of Abraham, who built an altar and called on the name of the Lord in response to God's promise (Gen. 12:8; 13:4). Later, Abram prayed in faith to God about an heir (15:1–6). The patriarch Job blessed God even in periods of adversity, pouring out the frustrations of his heart to God. He ultimately wound up interceding in prayer to God on behalf of the friends who had caused him so much grief. Moses communicated with God (Ex. 3:1–4:7) and interceded on behalf of God's people Israel (32:11–13, Num. 11:11–15). Joshua and the judges were led by God in response to prayer, and David's life and writings are filled with praise, petition, intercession, and confession. Solomon became the greatest king ever after praying to God for wisdom (1 Kings 3:5–9). His prayer of dedication of the temple (1 Kings 8) is a masterpiece of public prayer. The ministry of the prophets, such as Elijah and Elisha, was marked by miraculous responses to prayer, and the prophetic writings, especially Daniel, are permeated with the priority of prayer.

In the New Testament, Jesus' ministry provided both a clear example and consistent teaching about the importance of prayer. Matthew records Jesus' warning not to pray hypocritically but to communicate authentically with the heavenly Father (Matt. 6:5–6). Later, during a time when the disciples were struggling with their faith, Matthew relates how Jesus sent the multitudes away and withdrew privately to pray before coming to rescue the disciples in the midst of a storm-tossed sea (14:23–25). Later he notes Jesus praying for little children—an action the disciples sought to stop. And in those crucial last hours before His death, Jesus prayed alone in the Garden and invited His men to join Him in prayer (19:13; 26:36, 41).

Mark tells how, after the busiest day of His ministry, Jesus invested hours in prayer early the next morning in a solitary place (Mark 1:35). Later, Mark records Jesus' solitary prayer session between the miracle of feeding the five thousand and walking on the water (6:46) and His lesson on prayer, faith, and forgiveness during the final week of His life (11:24–25).

Luke, like Matthew and Mark, included the scene in the Garden of Gethsemane (Luke 22:40, 46, compare Mark 14:32, 38). But perhaps more than any other, Luke's gospel focuses on the role of prayer in the earthly life of Jesus. Luke identifies His praying with His baptism (Luke 3:21) and His withdrawal into the wilderness to pray during an incredibly busy ministry time when thousands were thronging after Him (5:15–16). In this and other instances, Jesus set a practical example for us of the importance of withdrawing from busy activities, good though they may be, in order to pray.

Later, Luke notes how Jesus spent an entire night in prayer before choosing His Twelve (6:12–13). The word Luke used to describe this was a technical term commonly used of an extended medical vigil—something a physician like Luke would have been familiar with. Later, Luke tells how Jesus took His inner circle of disciples—Peter, James, and John—into a mountain to pray, which is what He was doing when the Transfiguration took place (9:28–29). On another occasion as Jesus was praying, one of the disciples asked, "Lord, teach us to pray, as John also taught his disciples" (11:1).

Near the close of His ministry, Jesus told a parable about a persistent widow and an uncaring judge, urging His followers to always pray and never to give in to evil (Luke 18:1–8).

In another part of this discourse, Jesus called for authentic faith in prayer and illustrated His point with the story of the Pharisee and the tax collector (18:9–14).

At the beginning of His passion week, just after Jesus had entered the city of Jerusalem to the cries of "Hosanna! Blessed is the King of Israel," John records how He lifted His voice to His Father in the presence of His disciples at the Passover, "Now My soul is troubled, and what shall I say? 'Father, save Me from this hour'? But for this purpose I came to this hour. Father, glorify thy name" (John 12:27–28).

The disciples were privileged not only to hear this prayer of Jesus to His Father but also the confirming response from heaven, "I have both glorified it and will glorify it again" (v. 28). As Jesus explained, "This voice did not come because of Me, but for your sake."

## PRAYER IN THE CHURCH

Prayer played a key part in the early church from the very beginning. Following the dramatic response to Peter's preaching on Pentecost, the Jerusalem church continued steadfastly in the apostles' teaching, fellowship, the Lord's Table, and prayer (Acts 2:42). Peter and John healed a lame man who stopped them as they went into the temple at the hour of prayer (Acts 3:1). After being arrested and persecuted, they gathered with the company of believers to lift their voices to God in prayer (Acts 4:22).

Perhaps the strongest affirmation of the priority of prayer came when the Twelve gathered the multitude of disciples in Acts 6 to resolve the issue of caring for neglected widows. After appointing seven men to direct this important business, they noted, "We will give ourselves continually to prayer and to the ministry of the word" (Acts 6:4). This text served as the basis for the sermon preached at my ordination, and I have not forgotten the exhortation of Alden Gannett, the man who mentored me, to give myself as the apostles did to the priority of prayer and the ministry of the Word.

In this text we can see the two-lane "information superhighway" between us and the throne of grace in heaven. God's Word gives us the basic information we need, and we access God's grace and direction for every situation we face through prayer.

Peter himself continued faithfully in prayer (Acts 10:9), and Paul made intercessory prayer for those he taught a priority of his ministry (Phil. 1:9; Col. 1:9; 1 Thess. 5:23; 2 Thess. 1:11) and called on those to whom he ministered to pray for him (1 Thess. 5:25; 2 Thess. 3:1). Both the author of Hebrews and the apostle James emphasize the importance of prayer for believers (Heb. 13:18; James 5:13–16).

## CHRIST'S EXAMPLE OF INTERCESSION

Prayer is not only a major focus of Scripture, it was also a key component of Jesus' discipling activity with His men. The present tense the Lord used indicates that praying for His disciples was a characteristic of His life and implies that it would continue to be a priority even after He left them. In John 17:9 Jesus simply affirmed, "I pray for them." Later He added, "I do not pray for these alone, but also for those who will believe in Me through their word" (John 17:20). And that, friend, includes you and me. Think of that the next time you're struggling, feel confused, or have failed miserably. We have a Savior whose intercessory ministry specifically includes you. Just as He told Peter, "I have interceded for you," so He promises to intercede for us. In fact, the author of Hebrews says He "always lives" for that purpose (Heb. 7:25).

Furthermore, His intercession counters any charge that may be laid at our feet, any condemnation that we may face. Not only did His death provide for all our failures, He also continues to intercede on our behalf (Rom. 8:34). His intercession is part of the guarantee that nothing will ever separate us from the love of Christ. Furthermore, His intercessory ministry, plus His sacrificial death on the cross, provide us with all the defense we need before the court of heaven for any accusation, valid or exaggerated, that may be laid at our feet by the accuser of the brethren (1 John 2:1–2).

## THE CONTENT OF HIS PRAYER

The content of Jesus' intercessory prayer on behalf of His disciples is extremely specific. It contains none of the "God bless everybody" generalities that sometimes creep into our praying, and it demonstrates the reality of the Master's heart for these men. It is the same heart we must develop for those we disciple, and it can only be sharpened on the whetstone of prayer.

### Prayer for Unity

First, He prays that they might be unified in spirit and purpose, just as Jesus and His Father were. It is imperative that we experience the spiritual unity for which Jesus prayed. This is not an ecumenical or ecclesiastical union. Instead it is the intrinsic unity which Paul wrote about in Ephesians 4—the whole body of believers, joined and knit together in truth and love under the headship of Christ. It's easy for the pressures of a hostile world system to both distract us and divide us from our ultimate purpose of serving God and each other together. That's why Jesus prays that the Father will "keep" the believers—Christ wants us to experience unity in His body, the church.

On a practical level, such unity grows out of our loving God wholeheartedly and loving people unconditionally. It's the logical result when we obey Jesus' command to love God with all our heart and our neighbor as ourselves. Thus unity results as we exercise love, the "badge of discipleship" (John 13:34–35).

### Prayer for Protection

The second thing for which Jesus specifically prayed for His disciples was for their protection from the Evil One, Satan—the enemy of their souls and ours, "I do not pray that You should take them out of the world, but that You should keep them from the evil one" (v. 15).

The Lord fully recognized every factor that might stunt the spiritual development of these men and hinder their fulfilling the mission He would entrust to them. He was aware of the pressures of a world system geared to distract them from God. He also knew the weaknesses of their own flesh and the relentless efforts of the one Peter would later brand "a roaring lion, seeking whom he may devour" (1 Peter 5:8). So in verse 15 Jesus employed yet another word for "protection." The word He had used in verse 11, *tēreō*, usually means "obey" or "keep" in the sense of keeping commandments or the Sabbath. (Compare John 8:51–52; 9:16.) Here in John 17 it represents the idea of watchful protection, perhaps against the self-destructive influences of the world and the flesh. The word he uses here, *phulassō*, was a military term meaning to guard or protect against external attack.[12]

What a difference intercession can make at times when we need protection. One night a missionary and his companions were stranded away from their home and forced to camp on a hill. Since they were carrying money, they were fearful of an attack. They prayed together, then went to sleep. Months later a tribal chief was brought to the mission hospital. He asked the missionary if he had soldiers who guarded him that night they had camped on the hill. "We intended to rob you," he explained. "But we were afraid of the twenty-seven soldiers."[13]

Later when the missionary told the story in a church in his homeland, he was told, "We held a prayer meeting that night, and there were just twenty-seven of us present."

One of Satan's objectives, identified earlier by Jesus, is to "steal, kill, and destroy" (John 10:10). One of Satan's ways to kill people is by prompting them to commit suicide. One night a young man named Rueben got out of bed in the middle of the night intending to take his life. Miles away, his mother felt constrained to pray for her prodigal son. Instead of committing suicide, the young man eventually came to trust Christ. He became the well-known evangelist R. A. Torrey. Intercessory prayer, motivated by redemptive love, had protected him from spiritual disaster and death.[14]

### Prayer for Sanctification

A third thing for which Jesus prayed was their sanctification. "Sanctify them by Your truth. Your word is truth" (17:17). The concept of sanctification is one we often stumble over, thinking it to be somehow too complex or theologically mystical to understand. Actually it's a very simple concept, one you see illustrated every time you visit the supermarket. One evening as I headed for home after my radio program, I found myself craving a late-evening snack. I picked up two bags of potato chips at a nearby supermarket. As I went through the express checkout line, the clerk noticed that one of the bags wasn't sealed. Showing me the open hole, she asked, "Do you still want it?" "No," I replied, "I'll just take the one bag."

I noticed the same thing when I stopped at the drugstore to pick up my wife's special brand of nasal spray. The first package I picked up had been slit open, and there was no plastic seal over the plastic squeeze bottle.

The problem was the same in both instances. Neither the snacks nor the nasal spray were "sanctified." Each had become contaminated by the environment—at least the potential for contamination existed since the protective packaging was no longer intact. Jesus' prayer showed the importance of both intercession and God's Word—a subject He had already alluded to in verse 14—to protect them from the world's moral and spiritual pollution.

## Prayer for Those Being Discipled

A fourth and final emphasis in Jesus' prayer for His disciples can be seen in John 17:20–21. Here the Master broadened the scope of His prayer to include both His men and those they would bring to faith and in turn disciple. Again He prays for unity, the kind illustrated by the Son's relationship with the Father. It's this kind of unity that will attract a watching world to believe the message of the Gospel. Surely His prayer was aimed at preventing us from falling into the kind of petty strife, jealously, and bickering that so often characterizes believers today. Sadly, a high percentage of church splits occur, not over doctrinal or even moral issues, but rather over the kind of petty strife that often plagued the disciples as they debated over who would be the greatest in the kingdom. Jesus' prayer was that they—and we—would be freed from such things to focus on Christlike servanthood and effective ministry.

Perhaps one of the greatest examples of a specific answer to this prayer was Barnabas, the "son of encouragement." In Acts 11 Barnabas had been designated to play a key role as the leader of a growing new church in Antioch. Recognizing the task was beyond him, humanly speaking, he sought out Saul, a man he had mentored earlier. He brought him to Antioch and worked with him for about a year. Between them, the two men discipled many believers and ultimately "the disciples were first called Christians first in Antioch" (Acts 11:26). Their ministry team was first known as "Barnabas and Saul" (11:30; 12:25) but soon came to be known as "Paul and his company" (13:13) or "Paul and Barnabas" (v. 46). Barnabas was so committed to encouragement and Christlike unity that he didn't care whose name was first or who received the credit. It seems that there wasn't a jealous bone in his body!

A century or so ago, F. B. Meyer was pastoring Christ's Church in London about the same time G. Campbell Morgan pastored Westminster Chapel and Charles Spurgeon was at the Metropolitan Tabernacle. Both Morgan and Spurgeon often drew much larger audiences than Meyer. Troubled at first by envy, Meyer later confessed that only after he began praying for his colleagues did he experience peace of heart. "When I prayed for their success," he said, "the result was that God filled their churches so full that the overflow filled mine, and it has been full since."[15]

## THE CONCERN IN HIS PRAYER

When we turn from the content of Jesus' intercessory prayer for His disciples to the concern reflected in His prayer, we might ask, Why did He show such concern in praying for them? Ultimately, because they were, in a spiritual sense, the property of His Father. Now, most of us have a concern for our own property, and even for property that belongs to others. We want to take care of it.

Here's an illustration of this from our experience as grandparents. Last summer our daughter Donna entrusted her two sons, Chris and Albert, to us for a two-week visit. She and her husband were expecting a new baby—Brandon arrived in July—so it worked out easier during the final weeks of her pregnancy for the boys to visit us in Lincoln. We rearranged our schedules and made personal concern for the two boys a priority during that time. We did so because they belong to someone who is important to us—our daughter. But in a sense they also belong to us. We were especially delighted that during their visit Albert, age seven, came to trust the Lord Jesus as his personal Savior and began to take those first steps of growing in faith. His brother Chris had trusted Christ the year before at a family reunion. Needless to say, it was an exciting time for us.

Jesus had earlier discussed His relationship with the disciples as the Good Shepherd who would give His life for His sheep (John 10:11) and who would protect His sheep from Satan, the thief (v. 10a). As the Good Shepherd, Jesus knows His sheep intimately (v. 14), and they know Him, just as He knows the Father and the Father knows Him.

Afterward, Jesus explained these concepts to a crowd that had gathered on Solomon's porch in the temple, pointing out that those who refuse to believe in Him were not His.

> "My sheep hear My voice, and I know them, and they follow Me. And I give to them eternal life, and they shall never perish; neither shall anyone snatch them out of My hand. My Father, who has given them to Me, is greater than all; and no one is able to snatch them out of My Father's hand" (John 10:27–29).

Using these vivid images, Jesus outlined how He and His Father are related to His people. The Father entrusted them to the Son, who died to provide them with eternal life. So in one sense, Jesus' statement in verse 10 demonstrates that both the Father and the Son have full title, possession, and ownership, sharing the same interest in and responsibility for believers.

No wonder the Lord has such a vital concern for every detail in our lives! It's a concern He frequently expressed to His disciples during His earthly ministry. In Matthew 6 He spoke of the Father's care for their every need—food, clothing, even future needs (Matt. 6:25–34). Later, in the context of discussing their mission as disciples and their mandate to be like Him (Matt. 10:24–25), He reminded them that because of His protective care they need fear nothing. The same Father who omnisciently knows about a fallen sparrow and has numbered the hairs of each of our heads reminds us through His Son, "Do not fear therefore; you are of more value than many sparrows" (Matt. 10:29–31). These are marvelous reminders from Matthew of our Lord's total care, the same concern reflected in Jesus' prayer in John 17.

I'm reminded of another story told by Professor Hendricks of a man who sold his business and went into vocational Christian work. Family finances were extremely tight since there were four kids in the home. One night at family worship the youngest, Timmy, asked, "Daddy, do you think Jesus would mind if I asked Him for a shirt?"

"Of course not. Let's write that down in our prayer request book, Mother."

So she wrote down, "Shirt for Timmy." Then she added, "Size seven." You can be sure that every day Timmy saw to it that the family prayed for the shirt.

Several weeks later, the mother received a telephone call from a clothier in downtown Dallas, a Christian business-man. "I've just finished my July clearance sale, and I know you have four boys. It occurred to me you might have some use for something we have left. Could you use some boys' shirts?"

"What size?" she asked.

"Size seven."

"How many do you have left?" she asked.

"Twelve."

Now some of us may have been tempted to take the shirts, stick them in the bureau drawer, and just mention them ca-sually to the child. Not these parents.

That night as had been his custom, Timmy reminded, "Don't forget, let's pray for the shirt."

To which his mother replied, "Timmy, we don't have to pray for the shirt."

"How come?"

"The Lord has answered your prayer."

"He has?"

"Yes."

As previously arranged, his big brother went out, brought in one shirt and put it on the table. Little Timmy sat there, eyes like saucers. The big brother went out and brought in another shirt. Out and back, out and back, until he had piled twelve shirts on the table. By this time, as Professor. Hendricks put it, Timmy had become convinced God had gone into the shirt business! Today, there's a man named Timothy who learned in the most vivid way that there's a God in heaven who is interested enough in a boy's needs to provide him with shirts.

## THE CONSEQUENCE OF HIS PRAYER

Now that we've looked at the content of Jesus' prayer and the concern reflected in it, it's quite appropriate for us to consider the consequence or result of this intercession. It's a result He notes at the conclusion of His initial statement about praying. We might be tempted to pass over this statement lightly, yet it has great significance—"I am glorified in them" (John 17:10).

### Glorifying God

After all, the glory of God is the dominant theme of this section of John. Remember the opening words of Jesus' prayer, "Father, glorify Your Son, that Your Son also may glorify You" (v. 1). "I have glorified You on the earth" (v. 4). "Father, glorify Me together with Yourself, with the glory which I had with You before the world was" (v. 5).

The disciples have joined an incredible, glorious circle. The Father glorifies the Son, and the Son glorifies the Father. Anyone who is aware of the Old Testament remembers the Shechinah glory of God that first appeared to Abraham in Genesis 15. Moses saw it on Mount Sinai, and the Israelites experienced it in a pillar of cloud by day and fire by night. The Shechinah glory dwelt in the tabernacle, then in the temple, and ultimately departed from Israel (Ezek. 11:22–23).

John had been with Peter and James when they caught a glimpse of that glory surrounding Jesus on the Mount of Transfiguration. Now they hear that they themselves will share in reflecting God's glory in response to His intercession on their behalf. He further prays that they may join Him and "Behold My glory" (John 17:24).

In his writing, Paul looked forward to that ultimate glory (Rom. 8:18; 1 Cor. 15:40–43; 2 Cor. 4:17; Col. 1:27; 3:4). Yet He also recognized the importance of glorifying God in all the activities of our lives (1 Cor. 10:13). The routine things like eating and drinking, studying the Word, relating to people—all are to be done to the glory of God. As the apostle pointed out to the Ephesians, our past acceptance in God's family, in Jesus Christ, was "to the praise of His glory" (Eph. 1:6). Thus the purpose of our present lives (v. 12) and of our future destiny (v. 14) are also "to the praise of His glory."

Our commitment to the ministry of intercessory prayer, especially to those we disciple, is a step toward enabling them to more effectively glorify God.

Dr. Ralph Byron is an outstanding Christian surgeon.

Early in his medical profession he sought for a way to make his life count for Christ.

One day in his devotions he came across Ezekiel 22:30, "So I sought for a man among them who would make a wall, and stand in the gap before Me on behalf of the land, that I should not destroy it; but I found no one."

Dr. Byron pondered the question, "Would God find me standing in the gap?" He candidly had to respond negatively. As a young surgeon pressed with responsibilities, he concluded he had become too busy to become a true man of God. He needed to make prayer a greater priority in his life.[16]

At first it was difficult because of his numerous responsibilities. He decided that, to have the time with God for prayer and study of the Word, he would have to get up early. So he began getting up at 5:30 a.m., a time he referred to as "an unearthly hour."

But he did it, and it became the very best time in his very busy schedule.

Within two weeks, Ralph Byron discovered a quality in his spiritual life he'd never known before. Before long he had seen two men come to trust Christ. A major conflict in his church was resolved as he committed it faithfully to God in prayer.

His conclusion? "It was apparent to me that I must give prayer top priority—even if it meant getting six hours of sleep every night or less."

### Joy

We can see a second consequence of Jesus' intercessory prayer, one the Lord alluded to in John 17:13, "Now I come to you . . . that they may have My joy fulfilled in themselves." What an encouragement to remember that our Lord is concerned not only for His own glory but also for our experience of joy. He doesn't want our lives to be a grim existence, a dull, repetitive religious regimen. Instead He wants us to enjoy our lives in fellowship with Him.

The other day we received a book in the mail that reminded me of two phrases that normally would seem like an oxymoron but now fit together quite appropriately: seminary president . . . Harley Davidson

The common denominator is Chuck Swindoll, the new

president of Dallas Seminary. In his book *The Finishing Touch* Chuck tells the story of watching his youngest daughter ride off after her wedding on the back of a black and purple Harley Davidson Heritage Classic. Afterward, he went out and bought himself a 750–pound Harley Heritage Softtail Classic.

In his inimitable style, Chuck Swindoll raises the issue,

> "What's happening?" you may be asking. "What on earth would posses a man of my age to start messing around with a motorcycle? What is all this about?"
> What's it about? It's about forgetting the ridiculous idea that every single moment in life must be grim and sober. It's about breaking another thick and brittle mold of predictability. It's about enjoying a completely different slice of life . . . . It's about stepping into a tension-free, anxiety-free world where I feel the wind, smell the wild flowers, hug my wife, and laugh until I'm hoarse.[17]

Here is a rare bird riding on a rare bike—a man who takes God seriously but who doesn't mind laughing and experiencing the fullness of joy for which Jesus prayed for His disciples.

## SHOWING LEADERSHIP IN PRAYER

As the leader of His men, Jesus set the example in prayer. The same thing happened in the early church as the apostles gave themselves to prayer and the ministry of Word (Acts 6:4).

And it's what needs to happen in the body of Christ today.

When I was in college, I broke my wrist playing basketball. During my high school years, I had broken my other arm in a fall from a tree when a rope ladder broke. In both instances the broken bones had to be enclosed in a cast for a period of weeks—in one case, months. In each instance, when the cast was removed I discovered my arm to be far too weak for even ordinary tasks. It took time to regain my strength.

The same thing happens in the body of Christ. When church leaders fail to take the lead in prayer, ministry becomes powerless and ineffective. As E. M. Bounds once put it,

God needs, first of all, leaders in the church who will be first in prayer, men with whom prayer is habitual and characteristic, men who know the primacy of prayer.

But even more than a habit of prayer, more than prayer being characteristic of them, church leaders are to be men whose lives are made and molded by prayer, whose heart and life are made up of prayer. These are the men—and the only men—God can use in the furtherance of His kingdom and the implanting of His message in the hearts of men.[18]

I'm convinced that E. M. Bounds' passion for prayer has great relevance for believers today. Men and women who would effectively lead and disciple must be committed to prayer.

Howard Hendricks tells the story about the church in which he was involved that was having trouble finding a teacher for a junior high boys' class. Now I cut my teeth in ministry teaching boys—and junior high boys are a big challenge in more ways than one. As Hendricks explained it, "The list of prospects had only one name—and when they told me who it was I said, 'You've got to be kidding!' But I couldn't have been more wrong about that young man. He took the class and revolutionized it.

"I was so impressed I invited him home for lunch and asked him the secret of his success. The young man pulled out a little black book. On each page he had a small picture of one of the boys, and under the boy's name he had written comments like, 'Having trouble in arithmetic,' or 'Comes to church against parents' wishes,' or 'Would like to be a missionary someday, but doesn't think he has what it takes.'

"'I pray over these pages every day,' the young teacher explained. 'And I can hardly wait to come to church each Sunday to see what God has been doing in their lives.'"

What a Christlike approach to the ministry of intercessory prayer!

## SHARPENING OUR PRAYERS

Now what does all this mean to us? What are the implications for our ministry of intercession? Obviously, we must begin by making intercessory prayer a priority. If you have time to disciple people, you must take time to pray for them. And if you don't have time for either, you're traveling too fast and staying too busy. You need to slow down enough to savor the beauty and joy all around you.

Several years ago a newspaper story told how a new navy fighter jet shot itself down. Flying at supersonic speed, it ran into cannon shells it had fired only a few seconds before. It was definitely traveling too fast! Friend, you and I are traveling too fast when we don't have time to invest in prayer, to spend in reading the Word, to meditate on God, to worship with God's family, or to mentor others in the faith.

I remember some years ago when I was traveling through life a bit too fast, and a wise counselor advised me to take a weekend and do absolutely nothing. "Don't study," he said. "Don't engage in any kind of routine. Just get alone with yourself and God for a weekend. See what happens."

It was an amazing experience, and one I highly recommend. For you it could be the beginning of a reinvigorated walk with Lord and a renewed commitment to intercession.

Second, some of us may need to sharpen those long-neglected spiritual abilities like skill in handling the Word. Recently I attended a seminar where I heard Stephen Covey explain a concept he called "sharpening the saw" to develop personal skills. As Covey explained, "We're often so busy 'sawing' or producing results that we forget to 'sharpen our saw' to maintain or increase our capacity. Sometimes we become dull when we neglect physical well-being or fail to cultivate social or emotional relationships."[19] We become spiritually dull when we neglect such disciplines as time in the Word or a consistent prayer life.

It's crucial that we commit ourselves to developing, exercising, and stretching, following the example of our Master and ultimate mentor, the Lord Jesus, in this area.

I'd like to conclude this chapter with a few basic reminders about prayer. You've probably heard or read them before, but they are worth repeating.

First, we ask in Jesus' name, which means "based on His authority" (John 14:13–14). This isn't just tacking His name or a formula on the end of our prayers. It means we pray according to His will, based on His objective of glorifying the Father (17:4).

Second, we ask in faith, believing God will answer (Mark 11:22–24).

Third, we persist in asking even when we don't see immediate answers to our prayers (Luke 11:5–10; 18:1).

Fourth, we pray specifically (Phil. 4:6).

Finally, prayer should flow out of an abiding, daily relationship with the Savior (John 15:7). As the Lord promised, "If you abide in Me, and My words abide in you, you shall ask what you will, and it shall be done unto you." When it comes to the matter of intercession in the context of discipleship, perhaps we need to take the approach of Michael Jordan when he was asked about his return to the NBA. As he told NBC Sports, "It was time. I needed to just do it."

## ENDNOTES

1. As quoted by J. Oswald Sanders, *Prayer Power Unlimited* (Minneapolis: World Wide Publications, 1977), 53.
2. Warren Wiersbe, *Be Real* (Wheaton, Ill.: Victor, 1984), 180.
3. "Heart Trouble," *Moody Monthly* (January 1978): 70.
4. *The Bible Illustrator*, 2816.
5. E. M. Bounds, *Purpose in Prayer,* quoted in Paul Lee Tan, *The Encyclopedia of 7700 Illustrations* (Rockfield, Md.: Assurance Publishers, 1979), 1036.
6. *The Bible Illustrator*, 2816.
7. Ibid., 2816, 2841.
8. Ibid., 2841.
9. Quoted by E. M. Bounds, *The Possibility of Prayer* (Grand Rapids: Baker, 1979), 52.
10. *The Bible Illustrator*, 2816.
11. Ibid.
12. Frank E. Gaebelein, ed., *The Expositor's Bible Commentary*, vol. 9 (Grand Rapids: Zondervan, 1981), 164.
13. *The Bible Illustrator*, 2816.
14. Ibid.
15. Ibid., 1137, 1158.
16. Ibid., 603.
17. Charles Swindoll, *The Finishing Touch* (Dallas: Word, 1994), 37.
18. Bounds, *The Possibility of Prayer*, 52.
19. Author's notes from Stephen Covey's "First Things First" management seminar held in Lincoln, Nebraska, Fall, 1994.

# Chapter Eight

# DISCIPLESHIP STEP 4: ENCOURAGEMENT

"I kept them in Your name" (John 17:12).

The world we live in is a dangerous place. That's a bit of knowledge that comes early for most of us. Our parents warn us, "Don't talk to strangers." "Don't cross the street against the traffic." "Be sure to wash your hands before you eat—there are germs lurking everywhere."

The more we grow up, the more we come to understand the dangers around us. Violent crimes take the lives of innocent bystanders. Individuals are infected with AIDS, develop cancer, or come down with other serious diseases. Automobile and airplane crashes, hurricanes and tornadoes, and a dozen other causes—natural and man-made—make this beautiful world in which we live a frightening place.

In addition to physical dangers, there are emotional risks as well. Just the other day I was reading in our local newspaper about a long-term emotional trauma that had left lasting scars on the lives of several citizens of a small Nebraska community. The only thing they had done to incur this emotional trauma was to sit on the jury when a man was tried for the brutal murder of a young woman. They were shown pictures, forced to listen to testimony, and some of them even received threatening messages. Several reported they couldn't sleep at night. Some of the women found the sexual nature of this brutal crime caused them to turn away from physical intimacy in their marriages. Others felt extremely fragile emotionally.

Yet there are spiritual hazards that transcend the physical and emotional dangers of our world. Perhaps there is no other area in which the dangers are as great or varied. Even though life often seems peaceful, we live in a spiritual battlefield between the forces of heaven and the armies of hell. Sometimes our circumstances, much like those of Job, demonstrate the effects of a warfare we cannot see or are not aware of.

There are multiple ways Satan tries to put us at risk. The Bible calls him "the accuser of the brethren," and he seeks to slander us. He wages war on our thought life, using mental "strongholds" or false reasonings and beliefs to distract us and draw us away from the Lord. He seeks to create turmoil in our lives that will cause us to give up. From my experience as a pastor and my work with Christian counselors, I've become convinced that Satan often prompts individuals, including Christians, to take their own lives or to engage in other self-destructive behaviors. And of course the Prince of Darkness often transforms himself into an angel of light, motivating those who blatantly teach a false way of salvation or Christian living.

Another of our enemies is the world system Satan heads up. It's a system John warns us not to become enamored with (1 John 2:11), because it utilizes sexual temptation and other lusts of the flesh, materialism and the lust of the eyes, and the power struggles inherent in the pride of life to sap our spiritual vitality.

The third enemy is the flesh, the old nature's capacity to imitate Adam and disobey God, which still plagues each of us after salvation and even years of spiritual growth. The apostle Paul himself, mature and godly, honestly admitted his struggles with the flesh when he wrote to the Roman believers, "For what I am doing, I do not understand. For what I will to do, that I do not practice; but what I hate, that I do ... O wretched man that I am! Who will deliver me from this body of death?" (Rom. 7:15, 24).

## SHEEP AT RISK

As Jesus prayed to the Father the night before His crucifixion, He identified still another step in the ministry He had
fulfilled in the lives of these key men. He had been with them
in the world, selected them out of the world to be His special people, and now they belonged to Him.

Yet He was about to leave the world (John 17:11) while
they would remain in its dangerous, hostile environment.
Clearly a part of His intercessory prayer entreated His holy
Father to keep His men (v. 11). Then, in verse 12 He said,
"While I was with them in the world, I kept them in Your
Name. Those whom You gave Me, I have kept and none of
them is lost except the son of perdition that the Scripture
might be fulfilled."

The level of Jesus' concern for these men was extremely
high as He prepared to leave them, first for the cross, then
for heaven. He knew they would be exposed to the hostility
and the allure of a world that hated them (v. 14).

Earlier in His ministry, after He had healed a man who
had been blind from birth, Jesus took advantage of a dialog
with His critics, the Pharisees, to communicate to John and
the other disciples some of the dangers of the environment
in which they lived. He used one of the most familiar pictures in the Palestine of their day, that of a shepherd and his
sheep (10:1–16). In this passage Jesus pinpointed the danger of thieves and robbers who posed as shepherds, but who
really had no interest in the welfare of the sheep. The sheep
of Jesus' day faced danger not only from wolves but from
thieves and robbers who came "to steal, and to kill, and to
destroy" (v. 10). Although the disciples had trouble understanding what He was saying at the time, I think Jesus was
underscoring the danger of the teaching of the Pharisees,
scribes, and Sadducees when He pointed out, "All who came
before Me are thieves and robbers, but the sheep did not
hear them."

Clearly, one important part of the ministry of Jesus to His
disciples involved keeping or protecting them. His ministry of protection extended to the point of laying down His
life for the sheep (v. 15), and on it the guarantee of eternal
life rests (v. 28).

To a great extent this aspect of Jesus' discipling is unique to Him because of His person and relationship with His Father (vv. 29–30). After all, we are not omnipotent as Jesus is. We cannot guarantee the perseverance of those we disciple nor are we involved in giving them eternal life, as He did. Clearly this is a special facet of Jesus' ministry to His disciples and to the "other sheep" He has (vv. 16–17, 20–21).

Yet we have been called to disciple the Lord's sheep in a dangerous world. And while we cannot protect them in exactly the same way Jesus did, we can be used by the Holy Spirit to fulfill two very important functions which parallel the Lord's work with His men. These functions are encouragement and shepherding.

Some time ago I spoke at a church in northern Kansas. During my visit there, I had the opportunity to talk with a man named Roger Will. Few men know as much about sheep as Roger knows because he has given his life to shepherding. In fact, he explained several dangers faced by sheep, some of which he included in a tract he has written on the subject. He explains, "Sheep are my business. They are dumb, stubborn, and contrary—and have a rather offensive odor."

Roger explained that sheep are at risk of dying from several dozen hazards. These include bloat, overeating on grain, choking, hanging themselves or getting caught on a fence, not to mention many diseases, ticks, and numerous kinds of worms. Sheep can get turned upside down on their backs, or they can pile up and smother the sheep on the inside of the pile. They may be killed by coyotes or dogs.

According to Roger, mortality for lambs at birth is high due to both smothering and chilling. Ironically, Roger explained, since ewes identify their young by individual scent, it is possible to utilize a mother's milk supply even when her lamb dies. "We simply skin the dead lamb and place the pelt over an orphan. The color, size, and shape of the orphan are not important to the foster mother. Because of the covering, she usually accepts the lamb." According to Roger this procedure works about 80 percent of the time.

In his tract, Roger used this procedure to draw a parallel to a covering that gains acceptance 100 percent of the time— the death of the Lord Jesus Christ, the Lamb of God, whose sacrifice provided the covering of righteousness for us when we trust Him for salvation.

As we noted in the previous chapter, two different Greek

words are used to describe His care for His disciples and His asking the Father to protect them. First, in verse 11, He asked the Father to *keep* them through His name. This word generally has the idea of "observe" as it is used in John of observing the commandments (8:51–52) or the Sabbath (9:16). This word, *tēreō*, can be applied to people "in the sense of preserving with an implication of defense."[1] For the Father to keep Jesus' disciples in His name involved His watch-care over them based on the authority represented by His name. How encouraging for us to be reminded today that the same Father watches over us as well. He is the Father who watched over Israel and never dozed off on the job or fell asleep (Ps. 121:4).

In verse 12 Jesus used the same word for His own care for the disciples, then employed a synonym, *phylassō*, which was often used of a military guard against an external attack.

The word *phylassō* is used in several places in Scripture with the idea of guarding or protecting. It described the four squads of soldiers that guarded Peter (Acts 12:4), the guard under which Paul was kept in Herod's palace (23:25), and the guard attached to his residence in Rome (28:16). Jesus used it of the armed strong man who guarded his household (Luke 11:21). Perhaps the use that best illustrates what Jesus was describing in His prayer is Luke's account of the shepherds abiding in the fields at the time of Christ's birth, *keeping watch* over their flocks by night (2:8). Clearly they had a positive, protective purpose as they shepherded and encouraged their sheep through the dangerous nights and days.

In effect, what Jesus was saying is, "I've kept an eye on these men. I've guarded them, protected them from harm. Father, now that I've completed My 'watch' and I'm about to turn them over to You, I can account for all of them. Other than Judas Iscariot the son of perdition, who carried out the role We knew he would fulfill, they're all safe and accounted for."

## SHEPHERD AND ENCOURAGE

I believe our best option is to fulfill two important roles Jesus Himself fulfilled in the lives of these men—a shepherd and an encourager.

Jesus had already pointed out to the disciples His own shepherding ministry, guarding them against wolves and uncaring hirelings (John 10:11–14). He knew His sheep and was known by them. The disciples couldn't have missed the point of that statement.

Then in the Upper Room, as the Lord let His men know about His impending departure, He promised them "another Helper . . . the Spirit of Truth" (14:16–17). The disciples couldn't miss the impact of His statement here either since there were two words He could have used for "another." One, *allos,* means "another of the same kind" while the other term, *heteros,* "another of a different kind." The second term was the one employed by John the Baptist when, near the end of his life, he asked "Are You the Coming One, or do we look for another?" (Matt. 11:3). It was also used of Jesus' appearance in a different form to the two men on the road to Emmaus (Mark 16:12), when they were unable to recognize Him.

However, in the Upper Room (John 14), Jesus used *allos* to describe the Holy Spirit as a Comforter who would function as He did, who would be called alongside to help.

From what Jesus told these men in John 14:16, I conclude that a part of Jesus' "keeping ministry" toward the disciples involved His role as their encourager.

Because of both the biblical evidence and my own ministry experience, I am personally convinced that encouragement is one of the most essential ingredients for successful discipling. Far too often we have equated the discipleship process with spiritual authority, structured programs, or simply reading verses and learning God's Word together.

Just a few weeks ago I sat in a beautiful restaurant filled with polished wood and antiques in downtown Lincoln, drinking cappuccino and talking with John Hatfield. John is a staff trainer with the Navigators, and he has made discipling his life priority. During lunch John had been telling me about the four elements of his "TIDE" principle for discipling: teaching, involvement, discovery, and experience. As I listened, John told how he and his wife, Kathy, had implemented teaching opportunities, become personally involved in lives, challenged those they discipled to personal spiritual development and biblical discovery, and urged their disciples to put those things they learned into practice.

I asked John to tell me about the people who were involved in his life. "Were there individuals who discipled you, who impacted your life, that may have played a role in your becoming so passionate about discipleship?"

The look on John's face when I asked him that question reminded me of the sun coming from behind a cloud. He smiled broadly and said, "Don, there have been two key men in my life. One was Merlin. When I first became a Christian, he was just another student at Kansas State University. I think the key thing he did for me was that he loved me and accepted me just the way I was. I didn't have to perform; I didn't have to jump through hoops, nothing like that. Merlin built a relationship with me. He was transparent with his life. He came and helped in my Bible study, helped me in Scripture memory, listened to me, taught me to go out and do evangelism, taught me to pray."

After John had filled in some of the details about how Merlin discipled him, he proceeded to tell me about Ron Schimkus.

"I had graduated from K State and gone to Iowa State. Ron was my staff man at that time. There were about three to four hundred people involved in Navs at Iowa State, and you could see generational changes through the process of discipleship.

"Ron became my closest confidant. When Paul talked about having a 'kindred spirit' with Timothy in Philippians 2, that's the kind of relationship Ron and I have, even to this day. He knows every terrible detail of my life. He's discipled me for over fifteen years now. We have a close relationship. I lived in his home, we did ministry together. I bounced just about everything in my life off him. He's my accountability person; he loves me; his wife is involved with my wife. In fact, I've gotten my whole philosophy of disciple-making from Ron."

As I listened to John Hatfield tell about the two men who had discipled him, I kept coming back to an important common denominator. It was true that both Merlin and Ron had taught John the Word, motivated him to memorize Scripture, and given him direction. But perhaps the most important thing each had done was encourage him. They had been there, involved in his life and caring about him as a person. They had fulfilled that important role of encourager.

In a day when spiritual dangers lurk at every turn, I'm convinced that as much as anything, encouragement can help keep disciples from defecting.

Ironically, just as I finished writing the preceding paragraphs about John, the phone rang. It was Kara, a young lady for whom my wife, Kathy, has been a source of both discipleship and encouragement. In fact, Kathy and I have also shepherded Kara and her husband, Vern. We pastored them, taught them the Word, counseled with them through struggles in their marriage and during a time when they were seeking God's will in their lives concerning vocational Christian ministry.

It was obvious from the tone of Kara's voice that she felt discouraged. Just recently Kathy had spent some time talking with her, sensing that she felt like giving up. It is at such points that encouragement can play a key role. While we cannot guarantee that there will be no defections like Judas or denials like Peter, we can certainly be there for those struggling, hurting individuals to whom we minister.

Stanley Jones tells about a decisive moment in his life when he could have experienced a spiritual disaster. As he put it, "Suddenly I tripped, almost fell, pulled back this side of the sin, but was shaken and humiliated that I could come that close to sin."

Later, Jones went to a church meeting. While others spoke of joys and victories, he sat with tears rolling down his cheeks, heartbroken. After the others had spoken, the class leader, John Zink, said, "Now, Stanley, tell us what is the matter."

He told them he couldn't but asked that they pray for him. As he explained it, "Like one man they fell to their knees, and lifted me back to the bosom of God by faith and love.

"When we got up from our knees, I was reconciled to my Heavenly Father, to the group, and to myself . . . the estrangement was gone." As Jones explained, it had been a crucial point in his spiritual pilgrimage, one he described as "the moment when I lost music. My destiny was in the hands of that group. I was a very bruised reed; suppose they had broken me. I was a smoldering wick; suppose they had snuffed me out. Just a criticism, 'I told you so,' 'Too good to be true,' 'He was riding for a fall,' would have done it.

"But they never uttered a criticism, or even thought of one as far as I can see."[2]

How encouraging for us to know that, when we are tempted to succumb to the lust of the flesh, the lust of the eyes, or the pride of life, our Savior in heaven prays for us just as He as prayed for the men He discipled. We can be further encouraged when we know those who have mentored and discipled us in the faith are also praying for us.

## ELEMENTS OF ENCOURAGEMENT

Let's consider for a moment the parallel between encouragement and shepherding. The encourager is called alongside to help; the shepherd is to be there for the sheep, not deserting them. When I talked with Roger Will and in previous conversations with my friend Paul Heitzman of Lawrence, Kansas, who also raises sheep, I discovered there are key roles played by shepherds for sheep. Not only does the shepherd provide protection, he also provides food, shelter, and direction.

Consider the statements Jesus made about Himself as the Good Shepherd: "And when He brings out his own sheep, he goes before them; and the sheep follow him, for they know his voice" (John 10:4).

### Leadership

There are two elements in this statement involved in both shepherding and encouragement—direction and fellowship. The shepherd is a known quantity to his sheep. They don't respond to the voice of a stranger. There is a familiarity, an awareness of previous concern, that gives the shepherd the right to lead.

For many young Christians who begin a discipling relationship, this is one of the most difficult concepts to learn. It's also one of the reasons Paul urged the church not to "lay hands suddenly" on those who would be leaders. (1 Tim. 5:22). So often young people have the desire to lead but are unwilling to pay the price of investing as a servant in the lives of those they would lead.

Let's think back to the Upper Room. As the disciples reclined around the table, an intense discussion was underway. As we listen the subject shocks us. These men are actually debating who will be greatest in the kingdom! Then they fall silent as they notice their leader wrapped in a towel, basin in hand, washing their feet one by one, doing the job of the lowliest slave.

When He had finished, He pointedly urged them, "Follow this pattern, relate to others in the way I'm relating to you. Exercise servant leadership." If the quintessential leader, Jesus Himself, who provided the ultimate example of discipling, encouraged by being a servant leader—and it must have been encouraging to these men to have someone provide this kind of tangible care—then how can we do less?

Servant leaders who wish to effectively encourage in the process of discipling today may wash dishes, help repair a broken-down automobile, or run errands for someone who is ill. The New Testament encourages us to seize every opportunity to do good to those around us, especially to those who are of the household of faith (Gal. 6:10).

## Encouraging Words

Another important element of shepherding—and of encouragement—is to get to know the individual we're discipling. Some times we may have a tendency to simply pigeonhole people, to fit them into categories, to think we know certain things about them just because we have observed certain traits on a surface level.

However, effective encouragement and discipling involves getting to really know a person. Remember what John Hatfield said about Ron Schimkus—"He knows every terrible detail of my life."

There was one special incident John shared with me about the time when he and Kathy were ministering in Africa during a drought. "We were there half a year, and during the drought we only received water every other day. It was an incredibly difficult experience for us with children in diapers. Really hard.

"During that time, Ron really encouraged me. We'd talk on the phone; I would call him and literally cry and weep. When I was struggling, he immediately responded. Ron had been to Africa so he knew what we were going through. I'll never forget one of the statements he made: 'It's never as bad as you think it is, and it never was as good as you thought it was.'"

What an excellent example of encouragement and discipleship. Ron knew John, and he understood the situation—he had actually experienced what John and Kathy were going through. From that perspective he was able to share words of compassionate care.

In our Weekend of Encouragement Seminars, Kathy and I include sessions in which she talks about the role of a woman as an encourager, and I share about the role of a man. One of my major areas of focus with men is to point out how important it is to encourage verbally. Many men find it almost impossible to speak affirming, encouraging words, yet the book of Proverbs makes it clear just how important verbal affirmation and encouragement can be.

> Anxiety in the heart of man causes depression,
> But a good word makes it glad (Prov. 12:25).

When the anxious cares of life come pressing in like a flood, kind words can buoy our spirits.

> A wholesome tongue is a tree of life,
> But perverseness in it breaks the spirit (Prov. 15:4).

Here Solomon identified two important characteristics of an encouraging word; its intent is to heal rather than harm, and its nature is truth rather than deceit. Like the surgeon's scalpel or the dentist's drill, it may be painful medicine, but its ultimate goal is honest healing.

> Pleasant words are like a honeycomb
> Sweetness to the soul and health to the bones (Prov. 16:24).

There is both emotional and physical well-being to be gained from the encouragement of pleasant words. They are as enjoyable as one of my favorite childhood activities—chewing sweet honey right from the comb.

> Death and life are in the power of the tongue,
> And those who love it will eat its fruit (Prov. 18:21).

Without question words have an incredible power to harm or heal, to crush or lift up. They can literally hold the power of life and death! Furthermore, the use of the tongue is one major area where we always see the inexorable law of sowing and reaping.

> A word fitly spoken is like apples of gold
> In settings of silver (Prov. 25:11).

Finding the right words to say and saying them at the right time in the right setting is crucial. It is important for us to develop the skill of finding encouraging words and sharing them with good timing.

As I think about verbal encouragement, I reflect back over my years of ministry in live, call-in radio. My program, *Life Perspectives,* has been built around a mission statement of encouragement. What our listeners have received has been incredible help and reassurance by means of verbal encouragement—the right words said at the right time, with a compassionate, concerned tone and caring inflection. I think of Dr. Gary Oliver urging a man not to give up on his marriage, Larry Moyer patiently explaining to a frustrated caller how to share the Gospel with a relative in a different way, or Florence Littauer exhorting a battered wife to take action to break the cycle of abuse. Certainly as James reminded us, although the tongue may be one of the smallest parts of the body, it can have the same great impact on life that the rudder of a ship has on the direction the vessel takes.

How crucial it is for us to develop the ability to effectively communicate with caring words.

## Steadfastness

Another important trait of an encourager is steadfastness. Barnabas played a key role in more than a year of discipling and growth for the believers in Antioch (Acts 11:19–26). It was a period of great blessing, as many new believers came to faith in the city located some three hundred miles northwest of Jerusalem. When Barnabas arrived, he could have complained about all the work he had to do. Instead, Luke records that "he was glad" (v. 23) and began encouraging them that with steadfastness of heart they would cling to the Lord. That's the kind of discipling mixed with encouragement that Al Quie, Senator Hughes, and Doug Coe shared with newly converted Chuck Colson as they began gathering each Monday morning for breakfast, fellowship, study of the Word, and prayer. Ultimately the group encouraged Colson to invite beleaguered President Richard Nixon to meet with them, although the president declined. A similar invitation was extended to—and declined by—former Vice President Spiro Agnew.[3]

Unlike many who engage in discipling today, Barnabas' concern primarily focused on motivating those he mentored to follow the Lord. He urged them to cling to the Savior rather than to him—and his verbal encouragement was backed up by a consistent lifestyle (v. 24).

Finally, when he discovered there were more people to encourage than even he could manage, Barnabas took time out to go after Saul and get him involved in the process (vv. 25–26). The end result of their months of encouraging the saints in Antioch was that for the very first time the believers came to be called Christians—those who follow or belong to Christ! It was a watershed moment for the church, and it came about as a direct result of a long-term ministry of encouragement.

In the account of his Antioch ministry Barnabas shows yet another important trait of a world-class encourager— humility. When he first brought his young friend in the faith to work with him, they were known as "Barnabas and Saul." Before long the two men set off on an important missionary journey in Asia Minor (mostly modern-day Turkey). When they arrived in Antioch of Pisidia (13:4), they were asked to share a message of encouragement (v. 15). After Paul's message, Luke begins identifying the team as "Paul and Barnabas" (vv. 42–43).

What an amazing testimony to the humility and gracious character of Barnabas, the world-class encourager. He wasn't concerned about who received credit or whose name had first billing on the "marquee." His major focus was to get the job done. Recognizing Paul's unique gifts, he undoubtedly encouraged his colleague to take the lead.

## Forgiveness

There is one final trait that surfaces in the life of this world-class encourager, and it directly affects his discipling ministry. Barnabas believed in giving those who faltered or failed another chance. Both Paul and Barnabas had agreed to take an important young man named John Mark with them on their first missionary journey. Unfortunately (for reasons the Bible doesn't spell out), when the team reached Perga, John made the decision to turn back. Some time later, as they prepared to embark on a second missionary journey, Barnabas suggested they take John Mark. Paul sharply declined. As a result of their disagreement, Paul traveled with Silas, while Barnabas took John Mark (15:36–41).

While Bible interpreters disagree over the question who was right and who was wrong, it seems clear that world-class encouragers like Barnabas are willing to extend a second chance—which is what he did on behalf of John Mark.

### BARNABAS: ROLE MODEL OF ENCOURAGEMENT

When it comes to role models for encouragement, I don't think there's anyone better than Barnabas. While the Holy Spirit provides the ultimate role model for encouragement (and Jesus pointed out this aspect of the Spirit's ministry in the Upper Room), the man who gives flesh-and-blood perspective to the encouragement process is Barnabas.[4] I've labeled him a "world-class encourager" because like a world-class athlete, he is at the very top of his "game" of encouragement.

Originally, Barnabas was just plain "Joe"—he appears in Acts in chapter 4 as Joseph. He had been given the nickname Barnabas by the apostolic leaders, which literally means "son of encouragement." While many believers struggled to put food on the table, Joseph, the Levite from Cyprus who was now called Barnabas, sold the land he had inherited, took all the money, and sacrificially gave it to meet the needs of his fellow believers (Acts 4:36–37). From this example we see that generosity is one of the first traits of a concerned encourager—generosity with his funds, with his time, and with himself. Later, Paul would speak of the deep generosity of the church in Philippi and the fact that they first gave of themselves (2 Cor. 8:25). Both they and Barnabas had developed an amazing sensitivity to people and their needs.

Perhaps you've wondered, as I have, how Barnabas became this kind of person. Now we don't know for sure, but there is a possible clue that may shed some light on his amazing sensitivity.

Following Christ's ascension, the apostles appointed two candidates to fill the place of Judas Iscariot, the defector. One was chosen. The other, who was not chosen, Luke identifies as Joseph, called Barsabas (Acts 1:23–26). There are those who believe that this man Joseph was the same man whose name was later changed by the apostles to Barnabas. If so, his experience of rejection in not being chosen an apostle may have been used by the Lord to heighten his sensitivity to people who feel rejected and hurt.

In addition to generosity and sensitivity, this world-class encourager also demonstrated another important trait— loyalty. In Acts 9 when the believers' number one enemy, Saul of Tarsus, came to faith on the road to Damascus and was baptized in that city, he was the last person anyone expected to show up for Sunday worship at the church at Jerusalem. So it isn't surprising that when he returned to Jerusalem and tried to join himself to the saints, they were afraid of him and disbelieved his conversion (9:26). Not surprisingly, Barnabas was the man who acted—he brought Paul in and stood with him—and spoke up to affirm the validity of Paul's conversion.

When Chuck Colson first came to faith in Christ early one Friday morning as he stood alone on a Maine seashore, he didn't expect a whole crew of contemporary Barnabases to enter his life. But when he returned to Washington to face the Watergate special grand jury, he found encouragement from Tom Philips, Doug Coe—who dropped by his office unexpectedly to express support—Undersecretary of State Curtis Tarr, and several others.[5] Later, Senator Harold Hughes and Congressman Al Quie provided significant encouraging support. At a personal meeting, Colson recalled the words of Senator Hughes, whom he considered his political enemy. After Chuck had shared his testimony with a small group, he said, "That's all I need to know, Chuck. You have accepted Jesus and He has forgiven you. I do the same.

I love you now as my brother in Christ; I will stand with you, defend you anywhere, and trust you with anything I have."[6] As Colson went on to explain, after that meeting he no longer needed anyone to explain what fellowship meant or what Paul intended when he wrote, "Let us have warm affection for one another as between brothers" (Rom. 12:10).

Later, after Colson had been sentenced and while he was serving time in prison for his part in the Watergate scandal, he received a call from his attorney. Colson's son Chris had been arrested for possession of narcotics. Chuck would describe those days as the most difficult of his life.

Before long he received another call, this time from Al Quie, who said, "There's an old statute someone told me about. I'm going to ask the president if I can serve the rest of your term for you." It was an amazing offer—a Minnesota congressman with twenty years experience, the sixth ranking Republican in the House, one of the most respected public figures in Washington, willing to go to prison so Chuck Colson could be free to take care of his family.[7]

If you've never had the need for someone to stand in your corner when others are standing against you, you can't really grasp the positive impact of a loyal encourager. Chuck Colson knew what it was; I've been there, and I've known others who needed it.

## RESULTS OF ENCOURAGEMENT

Ironically, the same apostle Paul, who had been a harsh, hostile Pharisee and whose critical spirit may have still been in evidence when he turned thumbs down on the idea of taking John Mark along, ultimately became a gentle, compassionate encourager himself. Probably Barnabas had left his imprint on Paul since it would not be inaccurate to say that during the time they served together in Antioch, Barnabas was actually mentoring Paul. When the apostle wrote to encourage the church in Thessalonica, a church he had been involved in founding, he mentioned several important ministry traits that are crucial to effective encouragement and discipling.

First he pointed out, "We were gentle among you, just as a nursing mother cherishes her own children" (1 Thess. 2:7). The picture of a nursing mother caring for her offspring provides an amazing example of gentleness and sensitivity. It's quite a contrast to the man whose previous career had been marked by the rigidity and hostility of Pharisaism.

Furthermore, Paul demonstrated a compassionate transparency. "So, affectionately longing for you, we were well pleased to impart to you not only the gospel of God, but also our own lives, because you had become dear to us" (v. 8). Here was a man who could open his own soul, who was now willing to put his life on the line for fellow believers.

Furthermore, Paul pointed out, "For you remember, brethren, our labor and toil; for laboring night and day, that we might not be a burden to any of you" (v. 9). In his ministry, Paul's goal was to demonstrate integrity of motive and action plus a sincere willingness to pull his share of the load.

In addition, Paul pointed out the consistency of his conduct. "You are witnesses, and God also, how devoutly and justly and blamelessly we behaved ourselves among you who believe" (v. 10). Paul was a man who sought at every turn to demonstrate integrity in his lifestyle.

Finally, Paul became involved in the lives of each individual. "As you know how we exhorted and comforted, and charged every one of you, as a father does his own children, that you would walk worthy of God . . ." (vv. 11–12). Paul didn't just live encouragement, he verbalized it—and he did so, as he reminded the believers in Thessalonica, by becoming involved individually in their lives, sharing encouragement, cheerfulness, and, when needed, even correction and spiritual discipline. As he pointed out later in the letter, encouragement involves warning those who are out of order, cheering up the timid, helping the weak, and being patient with everyone (5:14).

Glen Carter is a youth pastor in central New Jersey. He serves in the church where he grew up, but he now enjoys a discipling relationship with his pastor, Bill Raws, and one of the elders in his church, Ron Kirk. I met Bill Raws many years ago at America's Keswick, a Bible conference center, where I've had the privilege of speaking on a number of occasions. Bill is a cheerful, outgoing man with a heart for God and a genuine interest in people. According to Glen Carter, Bill has been much more than a pastor to him. "When I came on staff, he became involved in my personal life. He has so much wisdom, and he and Ron Kirk, who is a layman who works on C-141s at a nearby air force base, meet with me every Saturday morning for breakfast. We started these meetings as a requirement for my education, but they've grown far beyond that."

When I asked him what was the most important ingredient in the discipling relationship, Glen didn't hesitate, "Encouragement. They've sacrificed time for me; they've shown me they care about me as a person. Because of that, I've learned to open up a lot more. Both their personalities are on the encouraging side, even though sometimes I've needed a kick in the pants, and they've been willing to give it to me. I wish we could have more time to spend together."

Effective discipleship must include encouragement and shepherding. These important essentials were modeled by the Savior, and they are essential for us to effectively build up those we disciple.

## ENDNOTES

1. Gaebelein, *The Expositor's Bible Commentary*, vol. 9, 164.
2. *The Bible Illustrator*, 3025–26.
3. For a detailed discussion of this, see my book *Friends in Deed* (Chicago: Moody, 1995), 87–88.
4. Charles W. Colson, *Born Again* (Old Tappan, N.J.: Chosen Books, 1976), 131–35.
5. Ibid., 150.
6. Ibid., 338.
7. Ibid., 154–55.

Chapter Nine

# DISCIPLESHIP STEP 5: EDIFICATION

"I have given them Thy Word" (John 17:14).

During my college and seminary years, there were two words that, perhaps more than any others, impacted the lives, shaped the fears, and changed the plans of my generation.

Viet Nam.

It was an undeclared war, but it was warfare nonetheless. Television brought it into the living rooms and dens of American families as no war had ever been brought home to our country. I never served in Viet Nam, although I had friends who did. I remember talking with one of them recently about what it was like.

"Don, it wasn't the physical conditions so much as it was knowing you were in enemy country. There were all these people around us, most of them smaller than us, some of them children, women, young boys—and any of them could be the enemy. I had a friend who stopped to help some people beside a road—he wound up losing a leg to a grenade. The guy standing next to him was killed outright. It could just as easily have been me."

## ENEMY TERRITORY

What my friend described could just as well apply to the follower of Jesus in the world in which we live today. As the Savior prayed for His men and attempted to prepare them for His impending departure, He expressed an intense concern that they experience the fullness of His joy even in a hostile world (John 17:13).

Now joy isn't something the average soldier experiences. In fact, few if any who served during World War II (where my dad was a marine in the Pacific theater), in the Korean conflict (where several men I know fought), in Viet Nam (where many of my contemporaries served), or in more recent skirmishes such as Granada, Panama, or Operation Desert Storm would describe their tours of duty as times of joy. The life of a soldier is one of hardship, danger, and rugged commitment. In many ways, the career of a soldier parallels that of a disciple. Soldiers need protection from their enemies, direction from their commander-in-chief, and weapons with which to fight.

As He prepared to return to His Father in heaven, Jesus explained that an important part of discipling His men involved providing them with just such a resource, one designed to let them know exactly what their commander-in-chief wanted them to do in every situation. It was a weapon that could provide them with both protection and firepower in the face of the enemy. That weapon is the Word of God.

Just a few verses before, Jesus had said, "I have given to them the words which You have given Me" (v. 8). Now He pointed out, "I have given them Your word" (John 17:14). As I mentioned previously, the word *rhēmata* used in verse 8 seems to look at a specific utterance or message, while *logos* (v. 14) appears to be a more comprehensive term, looking at the written revelation of God as a whole. I believe this is consistent with Jesus' use of the word in verse 6, where He says, "They have kept Your word," and in verse 17 where He says, "Your word is truth."

That's why I'm inclined to draw a distinction between Jesus' statements in verses 8 and 14. I don't think He is simply repeating Himself, especially when we consider the use of these two different terms, the sequence and order of these statements, and how they fit in with the other statements He makes about His work with His men. I'm convinced that in verse 8 Jesus had in view the specific message of the Gospel, the fact that He was God's Son, their Messiah and Savior. In verse 14 I believe He was speaking of the entire biblical revelation which He taught them throughout His earthly ministry.

The word *logos* is actually used several ways in John's Gospel. In the prologue or introductory remarks it refers to Jesus Himself, the Word who existed in the beginning with God, who was God, who came to be flesh, and who dwelt among us. Later it was used of Jesus' spoken word which is received and responded to (John 2:22; 4:41; 5:24). It was also used of the words from God (5:38; 14:24) and the written Word of God, the Old Testament Scripture (10:35; 15:25). There is no inconsistency in these uses of *logos* by John; instead, they are complementary aspects of a word that is rich in meaning.

We can look back, from our perspective, to see a fundamental unity between the Scriptures of the Old Testament, the words of Jesus, and the writings of the New Testament that demonstrates its authority. As Jesus presented His claim to be God's living Word, however, there was no such perspective to draw upon. Instead, He demonstrated an authority that was fundamentally different than that of the contemporary religious leaders and teachers—the scribes and Pharisees. They were fond of citing past rabbinical authorities in an effort to support their own interpretations. As a result, their teachings consisted of layer after layer of interpretive quotations which often obscured and, in many cases, changed the clear meaning of the Old Testament Scriptures.

Jesus' approach is illustrated best in the Sermon on the Mount when he compared their interpretations to His own—"You have heard it said . . . but I say to you. . . ." Many of Christ's listeners were astonished at the self-evident spiritual and moral authority of His teaching, yet that authority posed a direct challenge to the social and religious leadership of the so-called masters of the law. Their response was one of open hostility and simmering anger. Jesus' ministry of the Word brought the enemies out into the open; that same Word would become the disciples' defense in the spiritual battle ahead.

## STRENGTHENED FOR BATTLE

If any one thing could be said of Jesus' time with His men on earth, it was that He gave them God's Word. He communicated an incredible amount of Scripture to them during His teaching ministry. In fact, of Jesus' words recorded in the New Testament, "ten percent of the daily conversation of Jesus was Old Testament verses, literally quoted."[1]

During the three years they spent with Jesus, the disciples were given the Word in large doses in every conceivable situation. When they listened as He shared the message of the new birth with Nicodemus, they heard Him refer to Moses and the bronze serpent in the Old Testament (Num. 21:9). When challenged with the question of which is the greatest commandment, He pointed to two magnificent principles from the Old Testament from Deuteronomy 6:4–5 and Leviticus 19:18 that call for wholehearted love for God and unconditional love for people (Matt. 22:37–40; Mark 12:28–31). When challenged by the Pharisees as to when the kingdom of God would come, He warned of the coming of Messiah by pointing to the days of Noah and the times of Lot, Abraham's nephew (Luke 17:26, 29).

Jesus didn't saturate His daily communication and conduct with Scripture just to show off an intellectual knowledge of God's Word. Instead, the Lord's goal for us can be expressed in one word—sanctification. As He pointed to the disciples' identification with Him (John 17:16), the Savior prayed, "Sanctify them by Your truth. Your word is truth" (v. 17).

The word "sanctify" simply means to separate or set apart, usually for some specially good purpose or use.[2] Its derivative meaning is to "dedicate" or "consecrate" and then "to revere" or "purify." In essence, what Jesus was describing in His prayer is the process by which the Word of God provides us with an internal form of protection against the external effects of the hostile enemy territory through which we move.

Whenever soldiers are sent into combat today, they are first given a series of inoculations, designed to combat every conceivable form of infection they might be subject to in the country in which they will be fighting. The jungles of Viet Nam harbored the debilitating enemies of malaria and other tropical diseases. Soldiers could not carry out their mission without being exposed to these dangers, so some kind of internal inoculation was necessary. Without question, God's Word provides us with that spiritual inoculation we need in order to face the temptations and hazards of a hostile world system.

John and the other disciples most likely knew about how Jesus used Scripture to overcome temptation. Following His baptism, Jesus withdrew into the wilderness where He fasted forty days and nights. Afterward, Satan assaulted Jesus with three lines of temptation, each of which involved a misuse of legitimate needs or goals and demanded submission to Satan's authority rather than the Father's. In response to each temptation, Jesus turned to the Old Testament, specifically to the book of Deuteronomy. He quoted verses in which Moses addressed a specific situation in Israel and applied them to His situation.

Like Israel, Jesus underwent testing in the wilderness to underscore the importance of depending on His heavenly Father rather than living by bread alone (Deut. 8:3). Israel had tempted God, just as Satan challenged Jesus to do (6:16). Furthermore, Israel had been tempted to serve gods other than Jehovah, which is what Satan tried to convince Jesus to do (6:13–14). In every instance, the Master applied what God had told Israel through Moses to His own circumstance in order to withstand Satan's assault. Furthermore, when Satan tried to turn the Scripture against Jesus by misusing Psalm 91, the Lord countered with a clear general principle from Scripture, "You shall not tempt the Lord your God" (Matt. 4:7). Clearly Jesus didn't withdraw from contact or hide from a sinful world system. Nor does He intend for us to withdraw.

## THE COMBAT ZONE

Part of Jesus' point in His prayer was to show that "the world has hated them because they are not of the world, just as I am not of the world" (John 17:14). The apostle John used the term "world" in a variety of ways in John 17 to describe the planet on which we live (v. 5), the people that populate the planet (v. 18), and the order or system—the Greek word *cosmos* carries this idea—that stands in diametric opposition to God and His purposes (vv. 14–15). Earlier Jesus had warned His disciples, "The world hates you" (15:19), and "In the world you will have tribulation" (16:33). My friend Warren Wiersbe uses two vivid illustrations to show how the believer is "out of his element" in this world—an astronaut in outer space and a diver at the bottom of the sea. His definition of "the world," succinctly expressed, is "society organized without God and against God."[3]

At its head stands Satan, that creature so magnificently designed to bring God glory, but who so totally and thoroughly rebelled against God and became the enemy of the Creator, the Savior, and of believers as well. Jesus twice referred to him as "the prince of this world" (14:30; 15:11). It is no wonder that during Jesus' temptation, Satan offered Him "all the kingdoms of the world" (Matt. 4:8). As John would later write, "We know that we are of God, the whole world lies under the sway of the wicked one" (1 John 5:19).

Jesus' concern for His men as they faced living in this hostile environment can be seen from the fact that the Savior used the word "world" nineteen times in this chapter. It is only by God's Word that we understand the hostile attitude of the world toward God and the desperate need of Christians to "keep oneself unspotted by the world" (James 1:27). Just as soldiers in Operation Desert Storm were exposed to chemical and biological hazards of warfare and those who fought in Viet Nam were affected by both hostile people and the environment itself, so believers live in a world system filled with godless values, driven by sensual temptation, and marked by arrogant power struggles (1 John 2:16).

Jesus had prayed, "I have given them Your word; and the world has hated them because they are not of the world, just as I am not of the world" (John 17:14). Now He requested protection from Satan, the Evil One, but not isolation from the world (v. 15). Believers live in the world but not as a part of the world. His plan for us is not isolationistic monasticism nor an insulation from the reality of life and its pains like His enemies, the Pharisees, practiced. Nor does He desire that we live so closely aligned with the world's values and pursuits that we end up like Lot, whose exposure to the godless values and immoral standards of Sodom corrupted his own character and destroyed his family.

## A LIGHT IN THE DARKNESS

As He explained early in His ministry, His followers were to be the salt of the earth and the light of the world (Matt. 5:13–14). John frequently quoted Jesus' claim to be the Light of the World (1:9; 8:12; 9:5; 12:46). As His followers, we have a responsibility to dispel the world's darkness. Centuries before Christ, the psalmist pointed to God's Word as:

> Your word is a lamp to my feet
> And a light to my path (Ps. 119:105).

Years ago I was employed by a man who owned a service station and who also worked in a nearby coal mine. When he would return to the little two-pump gasoline station on Highway 78 in Forestdale, Alabama, after a day in the mine, Mr. Haygood would often still be wearing his miners' cap, on which a lamp had been mounted. I was fascinated by this strong-beamed "cap-light," and he often told me how essential it was as he worked hundreds of feet beneath the surface of the earth. If his lamp failed, a miner would not only be unable to dig coal, he might not be able to find his way to safety! As the miners' lamp provides light, direction, and protection from running into dangerous objects in a mine, so the Word of God sheds light on the believer's path in the darkness of the hostile world in which we live.

Furthermore, our world is filled with moral and spiritual pollution—everything from off-color jokes (which today are frequently told in the presence of both sexes, not just men) to observations and comments that counter biblical values, to dishonesty in business, gossip, and other morally and spiritually polluting influences. As Jerry Bridges warns, "The Bible is our best defense against this pollution. David said, 'How can a young man keep his way pure? By keeping it according to Thy Word' (Ps. 119:9). The Bible will cleanse our minds of the defilement of the world if we meditate on its teaching. It will also serve as a continual warning to us not to succumb to frequent temptations."[4]

Like Jerry Bridges, LeRoy Eims works with the Navigators. He points to the Bible as the source of spiritual food and nourishment desperately needed by believers, just like natural babies need regular feeding.[5] According to LeRoy, you can give a new believer spiritual food two ways. One is to teach him the Word, the other is to teach him to feed himself. "It wasn't till I met Waldren Scott that I learned the second way of feeding on the Word. My friends fed me from the Bible, but Scotty taught me to feed myself." According to LeRoy Eims, being taught was important, but learning to dig out answers from Scripture for himself was critical.

A recent conversation with Navigators staffer John Hatfield demonstrated the importance of this principle— and also underscored a danger. John told me how Merlin, the man who had impacted his life when both were students at Kansas State University, began helping him in Bible study, Scripture memory, and in the disciplines of Christian living. In addition, John's friend Ron helped him see the value of claiming the promises of God from Scripture in prayer.

As he sipped his coffee, John reminisced, "I'll never forget Matthew 18. I have a memory of this man who's with me. We're together, life on life, I've been sharing some things about the relationship with my dad, and how angry and hurt I felt from what had happened in my past. Ron just opened up Matthew 18 and went through the whole passage on forgiveness. I'll always remember sitting in that Hardee's restaurant in Ames, Iowa, weeping as Ron applied that passage. And I'll never forget that portion of Scripture as long as I live. It's one of the passages I now share with other men who are struggling with the pain of their relationship with their fathers.

"Here was a man who took the Word and used it in my life. I've had the privilege of sharing it with men at the Nebraska Student Union, using the same passage and going over the same principle. My wife has done the same thing to help women she disciples with self-image. She takes them to the Scripture and talks about how deeply God loves them and accepts them. God has used a passage in the Song of Solomon to help her in her personal struggles with self-image, and she's used it over and over again with younger women who struggle with the same thing."

As John talked about his wife, Kathy, I thought about my own wife and the women God had given her the opportunity to teach. Recently, during one of our sharing times, Kathy told me about how much she enjoyed studying the life of Christ and how much she looked forward to having the opportunity to teach it again. I thought about a number of women in various situations whose lives have been impacted by Christlike character traits Kathy had taught them and how she had been able to encourage them in the things of the Lord through Scripture.

I also thought of the men I've had the privilege of discipling as well as those who had mentored me in the faith. In each instance the Scriptures had played a key role. There were Alden Gannett and others. In my Bible college and seminary years, Charles Ryrie, Phil Hook, Howard Hendricks, Robert Lightner, and others at seminary had taught me the Scriptures. As I reflected on Jesus' use of Scripture in the lives of His men, I found my old, well-used copy of *The Savior and the Scriptures,* written by Dr. Lightner shortly before I met him at Dallas Seminary. It is well-marked and still contains the personal note and reference to John 17:17 which Dr. Lightner had written for me. In the book he pointed out, "Christ always assumed the unquestionable truthfulness and complete trustworthiness of the Holy Scriptures with divine fervency and frequency. He declared its final authority and absolute inviolability. The Savior's attitude toward Scripture, His purpose in using Scripture, His extensive use of Scripture, and His methods of interpretation and application, all portray His reverent regard for the Word of God."[6]

I also thought about the men who had met with me for personal study of the Word, application, and growth in Hillsboro, Texas, and Lake Charles, Louisiana; the men from my church and the Bible college students who met with me to study the Word in Kansas City; the group of men who asked me to disciple them and teach them in the Scriptures in Dallas; and the men I've had the opportunity to mentor in Lincoln. In each case, it was the power of God's Word applied to life that made the difference.

## DISCIPLESHIP DANGER

As John and I traded stories about the use of the Word in discipleship, we discovered a common area of agreement. Then we discussed the area of danger. John put it this way, "Sometimes I don't even like to use the word 'discipleship' anymore because people have so many different definitions of it. I'd rather use, 'life on life.' I'll ask, 'Are you in a life-on-life relationship?' People can't be put into a canned program. In some ways we've tried to mass produce discipleship, and that's not what it is.

"I've had people involved in my life for fifteen years; I've been involved in people's lives for up to fifteen years. There's a guy who came to Christ my first year at Iowa State, went to Uganda as a missionary, he's back now, and I'm still in his life. We get together every year for an all-nighter, just to catch up spiritually. It's a continual process."

As I nodded agreement to John's observations, I thought about my friend Hal Thompson, who has served as a missionary and discipler for many years in Mexico and the Rio Grande Valley in south Texas. Like John, Hal comes from a Navigator's background. He was shaped by a man who was willing to get into his life, impact him relationally, and share the Word in the process. Like John, Hal doesn't see discipleship as a program but as a life-on-life process of sharing God's Word.

I think it's so crucial for us to recognize today that discipleship isn't a specific program, a series of materials, or a specified time period. Certainly God can use programs and materials, but these are no more discipleship than the building in which we meet for worship on the Lord's Day is the church. These are simply facilitating materials designed to help the process of discipleship take place. To the degree that they do, they are effective; to the degree that they become the process itself, they are a hindrance to discipleship.

## JESUS' USE OF SCRIPTURE

Surrounded by His disciples, Jesus was walking through the temple courtyard, Solomon's Porch (John 10:22–23). John recorded the occasion, the Feast of Dedication, then added the observation that it was winter. One of John's frequently used ways of setting the atmosphere or mood for his narrative was to give time or seasonal references. Here his reference to winter not only stated the time of year but also alluded to the chilly climate of rejection toward Jesus— a climate reflected by the Jews' question, "How long do You keep us in doubt? If you are the Christ, tell us plainly."

In response, Jesus established three important premises. First, they had already rejected His clear testimony—backed up by His miraculous works—that He was the Messiah He claimed to be. Second, their rejection demonstrated that they had no part with His true disciples, the sheep who had come to trust in and follow Him and who were secure in His care. Third, and most important to the discussion, He, the person with whom they were speaking, was one with the Heavenly Father.

Contrary to the opinion of some liberal scholars, there was no question about what Jesus was claiming. They clearly understood Him to be claiming divinity, and they took up stones to stone Him for what they considered to be the capital offense of blasphemy (vv. 31, 33).

In response, Jesus used God's written Word as the authority for His claim. The Jewish religious authorities had based their case on the impossibility of a man being God, yet Jesus pointed out, "Is it not written in your law, 'I said, "you are gods"'? If He called them gods, to whom the word of God came (and the Scripture cannot be broken), do you say of Him whom the Father sanctified and sent into the world, 'You are blaspheming,' because I said, 'I am the Son of God'?" (John 10:34–36).

Although the main point of this heated discussion between Jesus and the religious leaders was His deity, this passage provides significant insight into Jesus' view of the written Scriptures of the Old Testament. Here He used three terms, "Your Law," "the Word of God," and "the Scripture." Clearly Jesus considered the Old Testament to be holy writing, originating from God, and communicating His revelation to men. His quote came from Psalm 82:6, a song of worship written by Asaph who called on God to judge and rule the earth.

Jesus' point was that since Scripture referred to these human judges as gods and children of the Most High, it was certainly not inconsistent with Scripture for Him as a man to be considered God. Twelve times John used the word "Scripture" or "holy writings" during the course of describing Jesus' earthly ministry, and both the singular and plural forms of the word frequently appear in the other three Gospels. Here on Solomon's Porch, discussing His Person and divinity, Jesus clearly affirmed that the Scripture cannot be broken—a point on which He and His critics should have agreed.

In our day, the issue of inerrancy has been hotly debated: "Do the Scriptures contain error?" "Can they, in effect, be broken?" Jesus' testimony was clearly, "No, they cannot. They can be trusted as given by God and without error."

Early in His ministry, following His first miracle in Cana of Galilee, the Master and the disciples went to Jerusalem for the Passover, and He cleaned out the merchandising in the temple (John 2:13–16). His actions reminded His disciples of the statement by the psalmist, "Zeal for Your house has eaten me up" (Ps. 69:9). In the aftermath of that confrontation, when the Jews challenged Him to show a sign, Jesus pointed to what later would be identified as the sign of Jonah. "Destroy this temple," He declared, "and in three days I will raise it up" (John 2:19). Neither His Jewish adversaries nor His disciples understood what He was saying at the time—in fact, the Jews pointed out that the temple had been under construction for almost five decades (v. 20).

Later, however, John noted that the disciples recalled what He had predicted and "believed the Scriptures and the word which Jesus had said" (v. 22). Thus Jesus' ministry to His disciples was designed to reinforce both their confidence and respect for the Scripture and their ability to see how Scripture pointed to Him.

Bob Brueggan, a pastor friend here in Lincoln, recently told me about how another mutual friend, Stuart Rothberg, had mentored him while both were stationed at an air force base in Nebraska. The two men had spent a great deal of time dialoguing over Scripture, and Bob recalled how Stuart had challenged him to memorize Scripture and encouraged him to cultivate the habit of studying the Word consistently. Ironically, the day Bob and I had lunch together and he told me about his relationship with Stu, I was scheduled to have Stuart on my radio call-in program, *Life Perspectives,* that very evening. When I told Stu about having lunch with Bob, he expressed delight in how God was using the man he had mentored to build a love for God's Word into the lives of others.

"It wasn't just that he taught me the Word," Bob had pointed out. "It was both his love for the Word and his personal involvement in my life that made such a significant difference. We did a lot of things together, and that's where we seemed to impact each other's lives."

Before Chuck Colson came to faith in Christ, he spent Monday morning meeting with key presidential leaders, charting the course of power for the Nixon administration.

After he came to faith, he began spending the early portion of Monday mornings studying Scripture and praying with four other men, including his former political enemy Senator Harold Hughes.[7] God's Word became the essential fuel of Colson's drive in life. Later, when Colson entered the minimum security prison facility at Maxwell Air Force Base at Montgomery, Alabama, he began studying the Navigators' "Design for Discipleship" Bible study course given him by Doug Coe. During those studies, Colson told how the Scriptures began to come alive to him and how he began to understand his new and intimate relationship with Jesus Christ for the very first time.[8] Later, when fellow Watergate cover-up participants Jeb Magruder, John Dean, and Herb Kalmbach were released and Colson remained imprisoned, he found encouragement from Psalm 37:7, "Rest in the Lord and wait patiently for Him." After the seemingly impossible delay in his release, after his son was arrested on a drug charge and friends Al Quie and Doug Coe volunteered to take his place in prison, it was then that Chuck Colson completely surrendered his life to the authority of Jesus Christ. Forty-eight hours later, he was released from prison. Already he had begun developing the idea for the ministry to prisoners he would later found.

### The Inerrancy of Scripture

When we examine the way Jesus used the Scriptures both before and with His disciples, we discover several things. First, He viewed Scripture both as without error and enduring. In the context of discussing prophetic events, He explained, "Heaven and earth will pass away, but My words will by no means pass away" (Matt. 24:35). Earlier He had pointed out, "It is easier for heaven and earth to pass away than for one tittle of the law to fail" (Luke 16:17). Clearly, writings that transcend creation must be supernatural in origin.

## The Authority of Scripture

Second, Jesus clearly viewed Scripture as authoritative. Over and over He referred to the Scriptures as "the commandment of God." During a confrontation with the Pharisees over ceremonial hand-washing, Jesus charged the Pharisees three times with laying aside the commandment of God (Mark 7:8–9, 13). He accused them of releasing the commandments to cling to their traditions (v. 8), rejecting or setting aside the commandments to pursue their traditions (v. 9), and rendering the Word of God inoperative through their handed-down traditions (v. 13). From Jesus' perspective, the Scriptures were not simply given to provide education. Rather, they were designed to impact lives, to speak authoritatively to every area of belief and practice.

This is the same position Paul took with his young protégé, Timothy. Writing near the end of his career, he reminded the young man he had discipled that "all Scripture is given by inspiration of God, and is profitable for doctrine, for reproof, for correction, for instruction in righteousness" (2 Tim. 3:16). From Paul's perspective, the unique nature of the Scriptures demanded diligent study to understand them (2:15) and communicate them to others (4:2).

## The Prophetic Nature of Scripture

There's a final aspect to Jesus' view of the Scriptures: He saw them as pointing prophetically to Him. Over and over, He used the phrase "that the Scriptures might be fulfilled." He pointed to fulfilled Scripture when He preached in the synagogue in His hometown of Nazareth (Luke 4:21), and at the feast in Jerusalem (John 7:38). He even reminded His disciples in the Upper Room that His betrayal would fulfill Scripture (13:18).

Throughout His ministry the Master emphasized how the Mosaic Law and the Old Testament writings spoke of Him (5:46; 5:39), and He pointed out to Nicodemus how the incident with the bronze serpent in the wilderness foreshadowed the time when He would be lifted up to provide life to those who looked in faith to Him (John 3:14, compare Num. 21:9).

His major indictment against the scribes and Pharisees

was their failure to obey what He referred to as the "weightier matters of the Law—justice, mercy, and faith" (Matt. 23:23). They had focused on external religious practices and neglected the heart-application of Scripture, and the Savior was quick to point out that Scripture demands obedience.

### The Importance of Scripture in Discipling

It's a lesson everyone who mentored me underscored time and again, and a lesson I've sought to pass along to all those I've had the privilege of mentoring.

LeRoy Eims described the principle this way: "Applying the Word of God is taking a portion of Scripture that speaks to your heart, meditating on it, and developing practical steps toward making it an integral part of your life."[9]

Like many of us, LeRoy had struggled with anger. "At times, I had a violent temper, whenever it flared up I would haul off and bash my fist into the nearest door. In spite of the fact that I often bloodied my knuckles and on one occasion had completely smashed a beautiful diamond and onyx ring my wife had given me, I couldn't seem to stop. And, yet, here was God's Word, 'Put off anger.' It was clear to me that this was not just some good advice given to the people at Colossi centuries ago; it was God speaking to me at that moment."[10] As he grasped just how specifically God's Word spoke to the area with which he struggled, LeRoy first made a covenant with God: He would begin working on this issue and persist in working on it.

Next, he committed Colossians 3:8 to memory and began reviewing it daily for a number of weeks. He prayed and asked God to bring this verse to mind whenever he faced the temptation to lose his temper. Finally, he asked his wife to hold him accountable and to pray for him. The result: "Colossians 3:8 became a part of my life and gradually God removed that sin from me."

Friend, that's a process that works. The Word does bring change to our lives. D. L. Moody was right; this book will keep us from sin, or sin will keep us from this book. And discipleship, to be effective, must build on the Word.

It's important as we consider our own use of Scripture in discipling to remember how the Master used it. Robert Lightner expressed it so clearly:

Christ took the Scriptures as His own life guide. He also found in the Scriptures His spiritual nourishment and sustenance. His lifework was performed under its inspiration, temptations resisted by its strength, life crises endured by its sustaining power. He lived, labored, suffered and died with a total commitment to its authority. The Savior in His person and word was so committed to and identified with the Scripture that He and the Scripture stand or fall together.[11]

While discipleship that teaches the Word apart from relationship is a mere academic exercise, discipleship without the Word is devoid of the specific content which has the power to change lives. That's why in its most basic form discipleship involves a relationship in which the Word is infused into a life with the goal of producing Christlike character.

## ENDNOTES

1. Harry Rimmer, *Internal Evidence of Inspiration* (Grand Rapids: Eerdmans, 1938), 227.
2. Gaebelein, *The Expositor's Bible Commentary,* vol. 9, 165.
3. Warren W. Wiersbe, *Listen! Jesus Is Praying* (Wheaton, Ill.: Tyndale, 1982), 88.
4. Jerry Bridges, *The Pursuit of Holiness* (Colorado Springs, Colo.: NavPress, 1978), 149–50.
5. Leroy Eims, *The Lost Art of Disciple Making* (Grand Rapids: Zondervan, 1978), 65.
6. Robert P. Lightner, *The Savior and the Scriptures* (Grand Rapids: Baker, 1966), 11.
7. Colson, *Born Again,* 154–55.
8. Ibid., 282–83.
9. Eims, *The Lost Art of Disciple Making,* 78.
10. Ibid., 79.
11. Lightner, *The Savior and the Scriptures,* 22.

# Chapter Ten

---

# DISCIPLESHIP STEP 6: EXTENSION

"I . . . have sent them into the world" (John 17:18).

The closing decade of the twentieth century has been a time of unparalleled affluence for many people, especially those of us who live in North America. Landon Jones, author of the book *Great Expectations: America and the Baby Boom Generation*, quotes pollster Daniel Yankelovich in defining our era as a time marked by "the psychology of entitlement."[1] Ours is an era when baby boomers, Generation Xers, and others have come to be motivated by feelings of entitlement, that somehow we not only have what our founding fathers referred to as the right to "life, liberty, and the pursuit of happiness," but we also have the right to a comfortable style of living and to having most, if not all, of our needs and many of our personal desires fulfilled.

To a great degree, this thinking has influenced the church as well. Consumer-focused churches, designed to attract people by meeting their needs, addressing their hurts, and giving them meaning and fulfillment, have become the order of the day. Televisions commercials, long after all they've left the airways, echo in our thoughts like mantras of materialism. McDonald's told us "We deserve a break today," and Burger King urged us to "Have it our way." Beer commercials urged us to "go for the gusto" and reminded us that we *can* have it all.

## A MISSION TO MINISTER

However, an examination of the ministry of Jesus and His mandate to His disciples reveals a focus that goes beyond simply meeting personal needs. Jesus made it clear in His prayer before His men that, just as the Father had sent Him, He was sending them into the world (v. 18). If one thing is clear from the life and ministry of Jesus Christ, it is that He didn't simply come to feed hungry multitudes, heal sick people, and encourage the downtrodden. This was part of His ministry, as He made clear in His sermon in the synagogue in the town of Nazareth where He grew up (Luke 4:16–19). He had come to fulfill the prophet Isaiah's prediction that He would heal the brokenhearted, preach deliverance to the captives, recover the sight of the blind, and bring liberty to the oppressed. Yet at the top of His priority list was to preach the acceptable year of the Lord, the Gospel (Isa. 61:1–2).

There are two important principles that grow out of this early announcement of the scope of Jesus' ministry. One is that He didn't neglect physical or emotional needs. He was aware of them, cared about the people who felt those needs, and became involved in a significant way in meeting those needs.

Second, and more important, His ministry went significantly beyond focusing on temporal needs, no matter how acute they may have been. Jesus' ultimate purpose was to reveal the Father and His life-giving provision to a world which, to a great degree, was unaware of its most basic need.

## DON'T LOSE FOCUS

There are significant implications for us today as we consider the needs of people. It isn't wrong for churches to be sensitive to the needs of those who hurt or provide attractive facilities or "seeker-sensitive" services and programs. However, if we focus simply on healing the hurting or attracting the curious, we are likely to miss the ultimate focus to which the Lord called His men and sent them forth—to complete the process for which He called them by beginning a new cycle of ministry. It was shortly after Jesus preached that sermon in the synagogue in Nazareth that He specifically called Peter (whose mother-in-law He had healed of the serious fever) to "catch men" (Luke 5:10).

Years ago when I was a student at Southeastern Bible College, I was introduced to Robert Coleman's landmark work on discipling, *The Master Plan of Evangelism,* a book that has had a profound impact on my ministry. In it he points out that "Jesus was always building up in His ministry to the time when His disciples would have to take over His work and go out into the world with the redeeming Gospel. This plan was progressively made clear as they followed Him."[2] Early on, they primarily observed His ministry, yet they received many clues as to the Lord's ultimate direction for their lives. One instance happened beside the Lake of Gennesaret (Galilee), as multitudes crowded around the Master to hear God's Word. Peter, Andrew, James, and John were washing their nets after a night of fishing—a night which had been particularly futile and frustrating, since these experienced professionals had caught absolutely nothing. As they washed their nets, the Master stepped into Simon's boat and asked him to put out a little from the land. They did so; Jesus taught the multitudes for a while, and then He said to Simon, "Launch out into the deep and let down your nets for a catch" (Luke 5:4).

We don't know what went through Peter's mind at this point, but we can probably surmise. "Lord, You may know a lot about preaching and the kingdom, but I'm a professional fisherman. It's the wrong time, and we had absolutely no success last night during the proper time." In effect, Peter's words reflected that kind of thinking. "Master, we have toiled all night and caught nothing; nevertheless at Your word I will let down the net" (v. 5).

The miracle that followed was designed to illustrate Jesus' ultimate authority over them and what they were doing and to demonstrate His ability to give fruitfulness and meaning to their activity. Luke records how they caught "a great number of fish" so that their net began to break and they were forced to signal their partners in the other boat to assist them. Peter fell at Jesus' knees and said, "Depart from me for I am a sinful man, O Lord" (v. 8). Peter's astonished response demonstrated just how powerfully this incident impacted him. Jesus' reply to Peter, undoubtedly also heard by Peter's fishing partners James and John, was "Do not be afraid. From now on you will catch men" (v. 10).

In this simple statement was a clear-cut mission, a life objective, that was to become the driving force during Jesus' time with these men and especially after He left them and returned to heaven. It was no wonder that once they brought their boats to land, "they forsook all and followed Him" (v. 11).

Later, following Jesus' resurrection, Peter felt tempted to return to fishing. Jesus provided almost an "instant replay" of this event to remind them that He was still the Lord, the One who empowered them and who had the authority to direct their lives, since they were His disciples (John 21:1–22). That incident included another fruitless, all-night fishing expedition, a daylight encounter with the Master that led to a massive catch of fish, followed by a spiritual lesson and a concluding mandate to "follow Me" (vv. 19, 22). It underscored the fact that these were men who had been sent on a mission that originated in God Himself—a mission that transcended simply attracting crowds or meeting needs.

Surely there is a lesson for the twentieth-century church as we consider this final step in the process, a step which also initiates a new cycle.

## TRAINING FUTURE GENERATIONS

As Jesus began His third tour of Galilee, He called the Twelve to Him and began to send them forth (Mark 6:7; Matt. 10:5; Luke 9:1–2). They had been with Him, watched Him, and even participated to some degree—baptizing some of those who had responded in faith to the Savior's message (John 4:2). Yet now they were given their own mandate and mission to "preach the kingdom of God." Their work included ministry to those who were sick and in spiritual bondage, yet the primary focus was on their gospel message. Just as a mother bird pushes her little ones out of the nest in order to help them learn to fly, so Jesus established the sending process He would later underscore in His prayer and repeat on the eve of His resurrection (17:18; 20:21).

In a sense this "sending process" or emphasis dominates and permeates the ministry of the Master to His men. A short time after He sent the Twelve on their initial mission, He sent "seventy others" two by two to witness for the Lord (Luke 10:1). Apparently, the initial ministry of the Twelve had born fruit and now they were sent out again as part of a larger group which had been gathered in part as a result of their ministry. Again the Master reminded them, as He had done earlier, that the harvest was great but the laborers few (v. 2). They were not only to pray for laborers, but to become part of the answer to their own prayers as they went. Furthermore, since the Master Himself had sent them, those who responded to them were ultimately responding to the Master and the Father (v. 16). The joyful success of their mission prompted Jesus Himself to rejoice in the Spirit, praising the Father for crafting such a wise plan that bypassed the world's wisdom, yet utilized spiritual babes to proclaim this eternal message (vv. 17–22).

Against the backdrop of His focus on the mission of the cross, Jesus prayed in the Upper Room, "I also have sent them into the world. And for their sakes I sanctify Myself, that they also may be sanctified by the truth" (vv. 18–19). Clearly, when Jesus spoke of sanctifying Himself, His words were not related in any way to a sin-issue in His perfect life. Rather, He spoke of being set apart to the mission for which He had been sent—a mission of revealing the Father and providing redemption through His upcoming death. At this point His goal was that they follow His example and allow the truth of His Word to set them apart so they could fulfill the mission to which He had called them.

## DON'T FORGET YOUR CALL

Following His dramatic resurrection—the event that was to have a transforming impact on the disciples—Jesus took the opportunity on at least four occasions to remind them that they had been sent forth to do His work.

The first such incident took place Easter evening when ten of the disciples were gathered in a locked upper room. Suddenly appearing in the midst of these fearful disciples, Jesus greeted them and showed them the scars in His hands and side—which prompted them to rejoice. Then He reminded them of the mandate they had heard Him prayerfully utter before His crucifixion, "Peace to you! As the Father has sent Me, I also send you" (20:21).

The word He used, *apostellō*, was a familiar and common Greek term and came from the word *apostellos* which "originally meant a naval expedition; later it referred to the commander of a naval force; and by New Testament times it could be used for any responsible person sent to do a particular task for the sender. Every day hundreds of apostles traveled across the Greek and Roman world. Ambassadors went to establish an outpost at a foreign court, businessmen were sent to open new branches, and Christian apostles fanned out to win and organize churches for their Lord."[3]

During my years in Bible college and seminary, I recall hearing some teachers make the claim that there was no place for apostles today. The only legitimate apostles were those who had seen the Lord firsthand. So I set out to investigate the word *apostellō* in my master's thesis.

I discovered there were two uses of this term in the New Testament. One referred to men who occupied an official capacity and who met the qualification of being eyewitnesses of Jesus. Yet the term was also used of men like Barnabas, Andronicus, and Junias (Acts 14:14; Rom. 16:7) who had simply been sent forth on a mission to spread God's message. Certainly Paul used the word of himself in this way and included it in list of functioning spiritual gifts for the Body of Christ (Eph. 4:11; 1 Cor. 12:28). In a sense, this kind of individual, a "team leader" like the commander of an expedition in the classical Greek sense, held responsibility for planting churches and discipling individuals for the Savior.[4] While only certain individuals who had been with the Savior during His earthly life could quality as "official eyewitness apostles," Paul, Barnabas, and others—including us today—have been sent forth to catch others, to disciple them and build them up the faith. It seems Paul himself exercised both of these apostle roles.

Not long after Jesus appeared in the Upper Room to remind His men of their mission, He reinforced His original mandate to Peter to reach others adding a threefold urging to "shepherd His sheep" (John 21:15–17).

Later, on a Galilee mountaintop, the Lord made discipling the focus of what we have come to call the Great Commission (Matt. 28:16–20). Here was a crystal-clear explanation of Jesus' plan to impact an entire world, and it included several significant "alls." First, all authority had been given to the Savior. Second, all nations were to be the focus of the discipling process. Third, all Jesus' teachings were to be included in the instructing process of discipleship. Finally, Jesus would be with them all the time, to the end of the age.

Then just before He ascended to the Father, Jesus reminded His followers that, just as He had fulfilled the
Father's will, they also were to fulfill His mandate by preaching His message of repentance and forgiveness of sins everywhere, beginning in Jerusalem and extending "to the
uttermost part of the earth" (Luke 24:48–49; Acts 1:8).

## A DRIVING PASSION TO DISCIPLE

Reaching out to desperately needy men and women with
the life-giving message of Christ was to be the passion for
those who followed the Lord then, as well as for us today. As
Coleman put it so succinctly, "Evangelism is not an optional
accessory to our life; it is the heartbeat of all that we are called
to be and do. It is the commission of the Church which gives
meaning to all else that is undertaken in the name of Christ."[5]

As my friend Larry Moyer, who has given his life to exercising the gift of evangelism and training others to evangelize, recently said on *Life Perspectives*, "Reaching lost sinners
is clearly close to the heart of God the Father and the Lord
Jesus. Doesn't it make sense that whatever is close to God's
heart ought to be close to ours as well?"

The book of Acts makes it clear just how passionately the
apostles gave themselves to this mission, beginning with Peter's
forceful message on the Day of Pentecost. That message grew
out of the testimony of the entire company to a massive crowd
in Jerusalem, and suddenly the ministry began to mushroom—
three thousand on Pentecost, five thousand a short time later
(Acts 4:4). It was a movement the authorities tried unsuccess-
fully to stop, because, as Peter and John were quick to point
out, they were on a mission for God that took precedence over
the authority of men. Furthermore, they couldn't help but
speak the things they had seen and heard (vv. 19–20). As they
prayed for courage to speak forth His Word, God answered and,
empowered by the Spirit, they continued to speak the Word
with boldness (vv. 29–31). Theirs was a mandate to "obey God
rather than men" (5:29), and they rejoiced in the privilege of
suffering shame for the name of the One they preached (v. 41).
So they continued consistently to teach and preach Jesus
Christ, both in the temple and in homes (v. 42).

Today we need that same kind of passion that drove them
to fulfill this ministry. One of the best modern examples of how

such passion can impact an individual and a church comes from the experience of Paul Johnston, a Minnesota pastor. Paul began his pastoral ministry at the age of twenty, planting a new church and seeking to "identify people's needs, build programs to meet those needs, then administrate those programs."[6] Before long, Paul realized the limits of just meeting people's needs or simply building a congregation. Instead, he developed a passion for a ministry built on and driven by biblical values. The first of these stated values was "We will be a contemporary and progressive evangelical church, intentionally committed to discipleship."[7] This statement of values and mission led to a restructured, "seeker-sensitive" worship designed to be both meaningful to believers and sensitive to those who might be attracted to the Gospel, with a focus on people rather than programs. As Paul put it, "We want people to become the Michael Jordans of Christianity. We want them to be impact players in their work and their homes and their neighborhoods. It's not that we want only the super talented, we want ordinary people to make a difference wherever they are."[8]

What a beautiful statement of passion and purpose, and one that certainly should motivate us today. Anyone who can relate to Michael Jordan's or Grant Hill's skill on the basketball court—the ability to elevate the skills of those around them, bring a winning attitude and the relentless drive to "go to the basket and finish," as the sportscasters like to put it—can recognize how they represent, in sports, what we want to see in the lives of people today in the church of Jesus Christ.

Sadly however, as Johnston points out, there are professing Christians who not only have not adopted this kind of passion for Christ but who actually seem to stand in the way of it. These include some with a consumer mentality, who seem more interested in drawing from the church whatever their needs and wishes are than becoming investors in the mission of the church. These individuals need to move from the first stage of "come and see" discipleship to a "go and tell" attitude. There are others who function as antagonists, seemingly more interested in introducing some other agenda, perhaps to further their own drive for power and influence. Still others are so caught up in their pain and dysfunction that, if allowed, they will actually "strangle the church's calling" and undermine God's purpose to relieve suffering—their own and that of others.

## BECOMING A "POINT PERSON"

Although I have never met Paul Johnston, Kathy and I have been a part of congregations in Dallas and in Lincoln with a similar focus, "seeker-sensitivity," and a commitment to discipleship. Our former pastor, Steve Stroope, has seen tremendous growth at Lake Pointe Baptist Church in Rowlett, Texas, in the last two decades, going from fifty people meeting in a bait house on the shores of Lake Ray Hubbard to an expanding ministry of thousands. Their mission statement focuses on impacting the Lake Ray Hubbard area to produce fully developing followers of Christ. The same kind of focus has marked the ministry of our current pastor, Mark Brunott, who has put together a team of individuals who are practically involved in evangelizing and discipling in the city of Lincoln and on the University of Nebraska campus.

It takes a "point person" for a church to adopt this kind of passion and mission. As Paul Johnston points out, "I've never seen strong values come out of a committee." Usually the senior pastor serves as that point person, or someone else in leadership may have this function.

The ministry I'm currently involved in, Back to the Bible, utilizes the medium of radio, as well as literature, biblical counseling, and world missions to fulfill a fourfold mission carefully crafted by our General Director and Bible Teacher, Woodrow Kroll, and based on the mission of the founder, Theodore Epp.

The sharply-focused vision of these individuals reminds me of an opposite premise: "If you aim at nothing, you'll hit the mark every time." Sadly, many Christians and churches are seeing this principle played out their in their lives.

As Warren Wiersbe, who served as the link between Theodore Epp and Woodrow Kroll at Back to the Bible, points out:

> Jesus finished the work the Father gave Him to do, but His Church has not yet finished the work that the Savior gave us to do. Our priorities are confused, we waste our financial and human resources on grandiose schemes that have little or no relationship to the commission God has given us. We are rearranging the furniture while the house is burning down. We are entertaining the saints while we ought to be evangelizing the sinners.[9]

When I was talking with John Hatfield, one of the "point people" for fulfilling this mandate in our church, I asked him about his efforts to "keep the cycle going" by sending new disciples. He told me about Clark, a man who came to Christ fifteen years earlier in a Bible study. "Right now, he and his wife are in a difficult missionary area, targeting a small people group in India. It's a really hard mission field," John said. "And I'll never forget, several years ago Clark asked, 'Are you still bringing out a world map and praying with guys over that?'

"I had to stop and think about what he was saying. Then I remembered—that was how I gained a heart for the world. One of the men who had discipled me used to bring out a world map when we all were together. We'd lay our hands on different countries, pray for those countries, and also pray that we would be willing to go.

"Clark told me, 'When I looked back, I realized that was where I started getting encouraged that God could use my life and I could go somewhere and serve in His army to bring others to Him.'" Unfortunately, many in the Body of Christ today still think of themselves as "an audience to be entertained rather than an army ready to march."[10]

## WHAT IT TAKES TO SOW SEEDS

After our move to Nebraska, we saw acre after acre of wheat, corn, and other kinds of grain standing in the late summer sun ready to be harvested. Throughout His ministry, Jesus used the image of a field of grain ready for harvest to highlight the need for this aspect of discipling. Jesus used this same image shortly after showing them personally how to reach a single outcast woman with the message of life and then turn that encounter into an opportunity to impact an entire village in Samaria (John 4:35–38). He climaxed His words by reminding them, "I sent you to reap" (v. 38).

Some time later, as He prepared to send His disciples forth, He reminded them, "The harvest truly is plentiful, but the laborers are few. Therefore pray the Lord of the harvest to send out laborers into His harvest" (Matt. 9:36–38). Two important observations can be drawn from this challenge. First, Jesus genuinely cared—He was gripped with compassion for these struggling individuals. Second, He saw His men as the solution. He challenged them to pray; then He told them to go (10:1).

In one of the major parables Jesus used to teach His disciples this truth, He explained that taking God's message to
the world was like a farmer sowing his seed. Often there
would be rejection, opposition, and obstacles. Yet some seed
would fall on good soil and produce a crop (Mark 4:3–8, 14–
20). The seed, the message of God, would be sown by those
who delivered God's Word, and the soil represented the
hearts of men. In the land of Palestine in Jesus' day, the sower
would scatter the seed over the soil before plowing the
ground. In the same way, God's message is to be scattered
across human hearts. Some of these hearts have become
hardened and reject the message; others are shallow and
the Word does not take root. In still others, the cares of life,
the deceitfulness of riches, and other issues choke out the
seed that has been planted.

However, the disciples were not to let this discourage
them, since some of the seed would take root in good soil
and bear fruit.

Our mandate is not to produce results but to sow the seed.
Then, when the opportunity presents itself, we can reap the
harvest.

### The Power of the Holy Spirit

And how can we do this? In His final words just before
His ascension, Jesus reminded His disciples of how the process is to work. First, it required power, the power of the
Holy Spirit. Jesus had instructed His disciples to wait for the
power of the Spirit, the Comforter, the One called alongside to help. He would live within each believer, empowering them to share their witness. In a sense Christians, as
lights in the world, are like an incandescent electric bulb or
a florescent tube. We give off light only to the degree that
power flows through us. The Spirit of God is the indwelling
source of power. As we allow Him to flow through us without resistance and maintain our contact with Him, then we
are able to share the light of Christ with others.

### A Focus on People

Second, even as the Spirit empowers us, we must recognize that the process involves people. Jesus said, "*You* shall

be My witnesses." His primary focus was not on a program, a plan, or a strategy. In the book of Acts, it was people who were involved in the faith, who were scattered by persecution, and "went about preaching the Word" (Acts 8:4). These individuals did not include the apostles. In fact, after the persecution the apostles remained in Jerusalem while men and women from all walks of life carried the message to every corner of the world. Each assumed personal responsibility to become involved in the proclamation. Won to Christ and trained by the apostles, they quickly became involved in sharing the Savior with others.

### Proclaiming Christ

The third aspect of this process is proclamation. Christ the Savior is Himself the focus of this proclamation. As He said, "You will be witnesses to *Me*." In 1995 our nation became preoccupied with a variety of trials, the most noteworthy of which was the long-running murder trial of O. J. Simpson. In such a procedure, what the court demands is witnesses, those who can tell from personal experience what they have seen and heard. That's exactly what Christ is looking for from us. He's not primarily asking us to learn how to debate atheists, agnostics, and skeptics, or to memorize answers to all the objections people have. We are simply called to be His witnesses. If we have come to know Him personally by placing trust in His death and resurrection, then we are in a position to share with others, as the disciples did, "what we have seen and heard" (4:20).

### A Place to Minister

Finally, there's the place to minister, and it's very simple—we start where we are, and we may wind up going to the ends of the earth. Jesus urged His disciples to begin right where they were in Jerusalem. Then they were to move out in ever-widening circles to Judea, Samaria, and ultimately to the ends of the earth. If we have come to faith in Christ and been discipled ourselves, it is imperative for us to start where we are. Friend, have you considered that individual maybe where you work or in your school who needs your discipling? What about that person in your place of business? Perhaps there's even someone in your own family who needs to hear the message of Christ and be built up in Him. Start where you are, in your Jerusalem.

Remember my "reluctant" lunch meeting with what became a discipling group? Two of them had an office in the same building where I was working. Another worked nearby. When the four of us met for lunch, the men were quick to tell me they wanted me to disciple them in the faith. Although I initially expressed reluctance because of my busy schedule, I soon realized this was just another way of God reminding me to "start right where I was." After all, it's the Lord's way of getting things done.

LeRoy Eims, a veteran of the discipling process, relates an imaginary story about Jesus' return to heaven at His ascension, and the excitement that event generated among the angels. In the story, one of the angels asks the Master, "What plan do You have to continue the work You began on earth?"

Jesus answered without hesitation, "I left it in the hands of the apostles."

Another angel asked, "But what if they fail?"

To which Jesus is said to have replied, "I have no other plan."[11]

It's only a story, but it certainly conveys a crucial point. The future of the Christian faith, humanly speaking, was vested with the disciples—and with the process of discipleship—and it's a process to which we have been called and sent.

### ENDNOTES

1. Landon Y. Jones, "The Baby Boomers," *Money* (March 1983): 58.
2. Robert E. Coleman, *The Master Plan of Evangelism* (Old Tappan, N.J.: Revell, 1963), 82.
3. Robert Brow, *The Church: An Organic Picture of Its Life and Mission* (Grand Rapids: Eerdmans, 1968), 93.
4. Ibid., 93–94.
5. Coleman, *The Master Plan of Evangelism*, 92.
6. Paul Johnston, "The Passion-Driven Church," *Leadership*, vol. 13, no. 2 (Spring 1992): 64–69.
7. Ibid., 64.
8. Ibid., 66.
9. Warren W. Wiersbe, *Listen! Jesus Is Praying*, 140.
10. Hull, *Jesus Christ, Disciple Maker*, 10.
11. Eims, *The Lost Art of Disciple Making*, 38.

# PART THREE

# DISCIPLING TODAY

L ife occurs in cycles. The seasons themselves give mute but ample testimony to the cyclical nature of life. When I began working on this book, I looked out my window at gray skies, falling snowflakes, and a lawn covered with white. As I near the end of the project, the sky is a beautiful shade of blue, the grass is green, and the weather is warm. It's Good Friday, and I've just taken a break from writing to go outside and help my wife put potting soil in the large pots in which she loves to plant beautiful flowers.

This section of the book focuses on the ultimate result of discipleship. That's exactly what Jesus did as He shifted His focus to those the disciples themselves would reach (John 17:30). We've already looked at the result of Jesus' process of discipleship, particularly in the preceding chapter. Now let's take it a step further as we examine some additional implications of Jesus' process of discipling for today.

Chapter Eleven

# THE ULTIMATE RESULT
# OF DISCIPLESHIP

Those who will believe in Me through their word. . . .
(John 17:20).

B uilding is an exciting process. It begins with a plan, re-
quires adequate provisions, takes place in an orderly
process—first the foundation, then the framework. Ultimately it fulfills a goal.

Perhaps the apostle Paul had this building process in
mind in Colossians 2:7 when he reminded those to whom
he had shared the Gospel to continue walking in faith, just
as they had received Christ Jesus. He had discipled them,
and he rejoiced in the order and discipline of their lives and
the solidity and steadfastness of their faith in Christ (2:5).
But he urged them to take root, to be built up and established in the faith, just as they had been taught.

As the disciples listened to Jesus' prayer, they heard His
thoughts on the six specific actions describing what He had
done for them. They have been the focus of His prayer to
this point, and undoubtedly this must have left them feel-
ing a measure of encouragement.

Now Jesus shifts the focus of His prayer. They continue
to be included, but He made it clear He is no longer praying
for them alone, but for "those who will believe in Me through

their word" (v. 20). That process began on the Day of Pentecost and extends through today. And it's as up-to-date as today's newspaper or television news report.

## WHERE DOES DISCIPLESHIP LEAD?

It seems to me that the thrust of this part of Jesus' prayer is to show where discipleship leads. What is its result? What impact does it have? Our tendency today is to evaluate many things on the basis of immediate impact. If it works, if it produces today, we keep it and we cultivate it. If it doesn't, we throw it out. Corporate strategies, business methods, advertising techniques, all pretty much take a pragmatic approach. If one basketball superstar can sell Nike shoes, then it stands to reason that another superstar can sell Reeboks. If Dave Thomas of Wendy's thinks a bacon double-cheese burger can produce, then before long, Burger King and Hardee's will be pushing a burger with cheese and bacon. And if a product comes along that doesn't work—like the "McRib"—it soon disappears from the menu.

So what about discipleship? As a process, does it stand the test of time? The answer is YES. First, because the Savior said it would, and second, because we see its results. As Jesus prayed, He viewed the disciples as both the foundation and the means by which His goals would be fulfilled following His departure.

Let's take a look again at the process and note the parallel between constructing buildings and discipling people.

First there has to be a plan. The builder of our home here in Lincoln decided on a plan he wanted to use to construct a house on a particular lot on Jennifer Drive in north Lincoln, on a hill from which the residents could view the city and the capitol building from their backyard. Then, once the building plan had been adopted, Kathy and I needed a plan for funding our new home. A construction loan had to be secured, and we had to obtain a mortgage when we purchased the house.

Then comes the actual construction process—first the foundation, then the framework, and ultimately the additional materials and detail.

So it has been with the church, the body of Christ, the household of faith.

Paul described the process when he wrote to the believers in Ephesus. He told them that through this process they had moved from foreigners and aliens to become fellow citizens with the saints and part of the household of God (Eph. 2:19). Furthermore, they were now part of God's building, being constructed on the foundation of the apostles and prophets, with Jesus Himself the capstone or chief cornerstone (v. 20), in whom the entire building, carefully framed together, was growing to become God's holy temple in which each individual had a share (vv. 21–22).

Looking over Paul's description of the process of building up of the church demonstrates a remarkable parallel with Jesus' process and result in discipleship. It also reminds me of the church building projects in which I've been involved.

## LAYING AN AUTHENTIC FOUNDATION

At the church I pastored in Lake Charles, Louisiana, we were severely restricted by the small white frame sanctuary and attached educational-fellowship building in which we met. In an amazing turn of events, God made it possible for us to trade our single acre of land for six acres immediately behind a soon-to-be built shopping center in the heart of our rapidly-growing community.

There was just one catch. Like much of southwestern Louisiana, the acreage was low and swampy. Thankfully, as part of our agreement, the man who owned the land we were trading for promised to "bring it up to grade." He was a believer, a member of another church in the community, and as he told me later, he had figured it would take about twenty loads of dirt to bring it "up to grade." Before he was done, his company had actually hauled 250 loads, more than ten times the amount of dirt we had estimated, to provide us with a firm foundation.

That building became my first church construction project as a pastor, and since we did a high percentage of the work ourselves, I learned a great deal about the building process. One of the lessons I learned early on was the importance of getting the foundation exactly right. As one of the men told me, "It's a lot easier to tear out lumber later. But you never want to take a sledge hammer and try to move your concrete foundation around or break it out and redo it."

So, with meticulous care, we made sure the foundation was exactly right. In the same way, the Lord Jesus provided that ultimate foundation on which His church, His body, was to be built.

Once the foundation was in place, we went through the exciting process of fabricating and hanging a series of steel H-beams. As the framework for our building, they would function like the early apostles, providing the nucleus around which every part of the building would ultimately rest. They provided the connection with the foundation and imparted strength and stability so the building could withstand the storms that would inevitably come. They also served as a significant unifying factor, since the wood purlings and studs which were bolted to the steel framework helped tie every element of the building together. They also provided stability as the finish elements were added, and the building as a whole stood as a testimony to the vitality and strength of the local church as a witness for Christ in the community.

Several years later I watched the same process take place as we constructed a multipurpose building at our church in suburban Kansas City. First the foundation was laid, then the framework of concrete block and steel constructed, and the insulation, drywall, and fixtures were put in place. Finally, the lengthy process was completed.

I think the building construction process provides a beautiful example of the ultimate result of discipleship as the Lord expressed it in His prayer in John 17:20–24.

## BUILDING AUTHENTIC UNITY

The initial focus of this part of Christ's prayer is on unity, "That they all may be one, as You, Father, are in Me, and I in You" (v. 21). When it comes to the subject of unity, unfortunately, we tend to be creatures of extreme. On the one hand, some who name the name of Christ have pushed for an ecumenical unity that ignores doctrinal distinctives to lump everyone together in structural or organizational fashion. I remember years ago hearing one of my professors at Dallas Seminary compare ecumenical unity to throwing several cats in a bag or tying two roosters together and hanging them over a clothesline. You can imagine how little unity would result from such action!

On the other hand, there are those whose attitude is to fight other Christians wherever they find them and find fault with everyone else in the body of Christ. It's almost as though they think they have the spiritual gift of division (which, by the way, cannot be found in any of the lists of spiritual gifts in the New Testament!).

What the Savior is looking for here is not ecumenical union, but corporate unification—a vital, living unity that models the union of the Father and the Son. That's how Jesus described it, "As You, Father, are in Me, and I in You; that they also be one in Us." This kind of authentic Christian unity is something we sorely need in the body of Christ today.

Such unity often reflects itself in evangelistic and discipleship purposes, cutting across denominational and organizational lines to produce salvation and growth. Two recent examples come to mind immediately, Billy Graham and Promise Keepers. Neither is perfect, and both have been criticized by many. Some of the criticisms have been justified. But both have also had their impact on the body a whole.

This past spring, Billy Graham preached at a crusade in a stadium in San Juan, Puerto Rico. Now in his seventies, he has probably presented the claims of Christ to more individuals, in person and through the media, than any other individual of all time—unless you count the writings of the apostle Paul. Over twenty years ago, I had the privilege of interviewing Mr. Graham for the secular radio station for which I worked. I vividly recall to this day the impact of his gracious spirit, his personal humility, and the fervency of his commitment to sharing Christ with the world. When he found out I was a believer and a student at Dallas Seminary, he used the occasion to encourage me to persist in ministry.

As he spoke at the San Juan Crusade, the same video crew which has taped several projects for Back to the Bible was working to distribute the crusade to more than one hundred countries. It was a monumental undertaking, an example of vision and purpose to declare Christ to a significant segment of our world.

No, not everyone agrees with all of Billy Graham's methods. Yet the clarity of his gospel message and the example of his personal integrity have gone virtually unchallenged throughout the years of his ministry. He has become a unifying factor in the body of Christ, one of the means by which a watching world can come to believe that God did indeed send Jesus Christ.

The second tool which has cut across denominational and even racial divisions in the church today has been Promise Keepers. I recall several years ago when John Trent and Gary Smalley were writing a book *The Hidden Value of a Man*.[1] They told our *Life Perspectives* radio audience about the vision of Coach Bill McCartney of the University of Colorado football team for a movement to bring men together to reinforce the promises involved in their commitment to God, their wives and families, and society as a whole. From an initial rally of less than two thousand came thirty thousand men, then more than double that number the following year. By 1995, Promise Keepers rallies were attended by hundreds of thousands from virtually every denomination and racial background, from all walks of life, all joined together to give testimony to the power of the Gospel of Christ to change men's lives. Yes, there have been calls to a stronger doctrinal emphasis, to a greater focus on teaching. But the impact on men has been undeniable.

I've had the opportunity of talking with many men who, after attending Promise Keepers rallies, have become stronger disciples of Christ, who have maintained their commitment to integrity in their marriages and their businesses, men whose lives have been transformed into stronger, more positive witnesses for Christ. Many have reached out in love and reconciliation across racial boundaries to demonstrate "the unity of the Spirit in the bond of peace" to a watching world.

## DEMONSTRATING AUTHENTIC LOVE

Jesus had already reminded His disciples that the ultimate badge of discipleship was love. Down through the centuries Jesus example of love can be seen in the lives of others. Shortly before his death, highly respected apologist Francis Schaeffer pointed out two examples of how the world could witness the loving unity of believers.[2] In the first, two Brethren groups in Germany found themselves divided immediately after World War II over how they had responded to Hitler's forced union of all the religious groups in Germany. One group had accepted the Führer's edict, the other refused. The elders of the two groups met together to try to reestablish unity. Francis Schaeffer asked a man from one of the delegations, "What did you do?" and he said, "I'll tell you what we did. We came together and set aside several days in which each man would search his own heart. There was a real difference. The emotions were deeply, deeply stirred. My father had gone to the concentration camp. My mother was dragged away. These things were not just little pebbles on the beach, they reached into the deep wellspring of human emotions. But these people understood the command of Christ. . . . And for several days every man did nothing except search his own heart concerning his own failures and the commands of Christ. Then we met together."

Schaeffer asked the man what happened then, and he said, "We were just one." Unity was restored after intense, soul-searching prayer.

In the second example, Schaeffer told of a church in a large midwestern city in the United States, which included a number of traditional people from a community and a group of people referred to as "long-haired ones and the far-out people they brought." After trying for a time to work together, the church leaders met and decided to form two churches. They made it very plain they were not dividing because of differences in doctrine, but as a matter of practicability. The two churches supported each other, worked together, and conscientiously sought to practice love toward each other. As Schaeffer concluded, "Here is a lack of organization unity that is a true love and unity that the world may observe 'The Father has sent the Son'!"[3]

## GROWING TOWARD AUTHENTIC MATURITY

There are many tools being used by the Master today to unify the body of Christ. I've seen Christian radio in general and our ministry, Back to the Bible, in particular provide the same kind of impact. We receive letters from virtually all over the world, from individuals who have come to the Savior, who've been built up in the faith, associated with a local church, and even reproduced their faith in the lives of others who were initially impacted through Back to the Bible.

Some time ago when I was speaking in a church in Arkansas, a lady came up during a break in the seminar and said, "I was the pastor's wife here for a number of years. My husband went to be with the Lord some time ago. I want you to know that I came to personal faith in Christ through the ministry of Theodore Epp and Back to the Bible. My entire ministry has been built on that foundation."

Here is an example of how vital individual maturity has grown from these forces for authentic unity. And for that Jesus prayed as well. To this end, He said, "And the glory which You gave Me I have given them, that they may be one just as We are one" (v. 22).

Those church building projects in which I was involved each demonstrated a unity of purpose—different materials, different sizes and shapes, put together in different ways, but all tied together to achieve the purpose of the building. In the same way each individual component—each electrical cable and sheet of drywall, each plumbing fixture and each nail—had its particular role. The picture is one of both unity and diversity, ultimately leading to fulfillment of purpose—in the case of the church, reflecting His glory.

## GLORIFYING CHRIST

Jesus' references to the Father's glory take us back to the beginning of the chapter where He prayed, "I have glorified You on the earth . . . And now, O Father, glorify Me together with Yourself, with the glory which I had with You before the world was" (vv. 4–5). Some time ago I was talking with my colleague Allen Bean, our chief researcher at Back to the Bible. Allen has invested many years in studying and teaching God's Word. He sees the concept of "glorify" from the viewpoint of revealing what God is like—His love, His compassion, His forgiveness, His other attributes. That's what Jesus did, first to His disciples, then to the world as a whole. Allen noted that one of the reasons God changed people's names in the Bible (Abram to Abraham, Jacob to Israel) was to show how their character had changed. Allen and I agreed that, since God's name had never changed, both Jesus' purpose and ours was to reveal the unchanging character reflected in the name of God.

In John 15:8 Jesus had pointed out, "By this My Father is glorified, that you bear much fruit; so you will be My disciples." As Allen and I talked about discipling, we acknowledged a close connection between discipling, fruit-bearing, and glorifying or making known the character of God.

The process of bearing fruit in Scripture seems to point to three specific areas. One is the fruit of the Spirit, listed by Paul in Galatians 5:22–23, and including love, joy, peace, patience, kindness, goodness, faithfulness, gentleness, and self-control. As we are empowered by God's indwelling Spirit, we increasingly demonstrate these character virtues to a watching world.

The second area of fruit involves winning men and women to faith in Christ. This seems to be Paul's point in Romans 1:13 when he reminded his readers that he had been hindered from coming to Rome thus far so that he might "have some fruit among you also, just as among the other Gentiles." Wherever Paul traveled, his goal was to win men and women to faith in the Lord Jesus, and he viewed this as fruit.

The third area of fruit identified by Paul is the fruit of good works. One example he cited was the collection taken for the poor saints in Jerusalem, which had been given by the churches in Achaia and Macedonia (Rom. 15:28). Such fruit seems to include fruitfulness in every kind of good work (Col. 1:10).

As we individually glorify Christ by bearing fruit and as we sustain the process through discipling, the body is built up, and individuals mature as well. Jesus' goal is to see the entire body built into a perfect and mature whole to provide a clear-cut testimony of His saving grace (John 17:23).

Both authentic unity and vital maturity are included in Paul's description of the function of the church in Ephesians 2. They are being built on "the foundation of the apostles and prophets, Jesus Christ Himself being the chief cornerstone, in whom the whole building, being filled together, grows into a holy temple in the Lord" (Eph. 2:20–21). It's a vivid picture, one with which anyone who has watched an office building, a home, or a church building under construction can identify.

There is also the individual aspect of maturity, to which Paul points in Ephesians 2:22, "In whom you are also being built together for a dwelling place of God in the Spirit." The structure is being built together as God places individual believers into place and they mature. So each of us individually becomes the mortar or the bricks or the fixtures, the building components of which the body of Christ, the testimony to the world community, is composed. The Holy Spirit indwells each individual believer (Rom. 8:9, 11), thus each of us is a temple of the Spirit, designed to produce His fruit.

A classic example of how this individual process takes place can be seen in the relationship between Paul—who wrote the letter to the Ephesian church—and Timothy, the man he referred to as his son in the faith (1 Tim. 1:2).

Paul reminded Timothy that he had been sent forth by Christ as an apostle, to proclaim the hope of Jesus (v. 1). He pointed to Christ as the One who placed him in ministry and who enabled him to carry it out successfully (v. 12); then he explained how he had sought to set an example or pattern to attract others to Christ (v. 16).

Out of this relationship flowed the responsibility to glorify the sovereign God (v. 17) and a charge to Timothy to take personal responsibility as part of the body of Christ by demonstrating authentic faith and a good conscience (vv. 18–19).

The requirements for fulfilling this charge to personal growth in the faith were spelled out for Timothy later in the letter. Paul called on Timothy to live as an example of the believers (4:12), to personally teach and encourage others in the faith (vv. 11, 13), and to make use of his spiritual gifts to build up the body (v. 14). By giving personal diligence to his own growth and integrity, he would be able to impact others as well (vv. 15–16).

Then in the final letter Paul wrote, the apostle spelled out in clear fashion how the "chain of discipleship" was to work, reminding Timothy of his relationship to Paul as a son in the faith (2:1). He then wrote, "And the things that you have heard from me among many witnesses, commit these to faithful men who will be able to teach others also" (2:2). Paul's goal for Timothy was that the young man become a vessel of honor, glorifying the Lord (v. 21). Using a variety of images from everyday life—a teacher, soldier, a farmer, an athlete, a workman, a student—Paul urged Timothy to fulfill his individual ministry and calling to discipleship just as Paul had taught him (compare 2 Tim. 3:14).

## THE CHAIN OF DISCIPLESHIP

Paul identified a four-generation chain of discipleship beginning with the apostle himself, then Timothy, faithful men, and others. The apostle himself had been encouraged and mentored by Barnabas, even though he received a great deal of what he learned directly from God.

Without question, Paul considered Timothy a very special young man, and it mattered a great deal to the apostle that Timothy carry out the ministry to which he had been called. Paul's ultimate desire was to stir up Timothy's passion for service so he would exercise his spiritual gift while not giving in to timidity and fear (1:6–7). In a sense, Paul's "chain of discipleship" could be compared to a mile relay. Paul recognized the possibility that the second man in the chain could quit on the backstretch. So what he says to Timothy is, "Son, you don't have the option to quit. You need to continue going for it, enduring hardship like a soldier, playing by the rules like an athlete, patiently working like a farmer, mentoring others as a teacher. In short, you must work to pass the baton of your faith on to others." Interestingly, Paul encouraged Timothy not to mentor just one, but many.

In one of the last messages before his death in 1956, Navigators' founder Dawson Trotman told the story of meeting with twenty-five German men for three hours, laying out the Great Commission. After several of the men had said, "Mr. Trotman, you in America have never had an occupation force in your land. You don't know what it is to have soldiers from another country roaming your streets. Our souls are not our own." Dawson Trotman responded by reminding the men that Roman soldiers occupied Palestine at the time Jesus and His disciples lived.

"It dawned on me that when Christ sent out His men, they were in a situation so bad there could never be a worse one. There were no printing presses, no automobiles, no radios, no televisions, no telephones, no church buildings. He left them with nothing but a job to do. With it He said, 'All power is given to Me in heaven and in earth. Go ye therefore and make disciples.'"[4]

We need to make sure, however, that we don't foster an over-dependence on the one who disciples. Discipleship was designed to produce individuals capable of functioning independently and interdependently in reaching out to others. In some discipleship programs people become so attached to the people they work with that they can't really go out and replicate the process in the lives of others. The difference in results is like someone who's wired to a heart machine in a hospital and someone who's been implanted with a pacemaker. In a sense the person who disciples is like the surgeon who has a patient with an erratic heartbeat and implants a pacemaker. There may be periodic contact with the surgeon, but it's not necessary for him or the support system to always be connected. The individual disciple is not wired up, but wherever he goes, the pacemaker the surgeon has implanted is present, regulating the individual's life. In a sense that's how the process of discipleship should work today.

## THE ULTIMATE GLORY

Finally, the Savior expressed a strong desire to the Father to have these men reunited with Himself. Looking beyond their coming separation at His death and even the lengthier separation occasioned by His ascension into heaven, He prayed, "I desire that they also whom You gave Me may be with Me where I am, that they may behold My glory which You have given Me" (v. 24).

It may be hard for us to use the eternal glory of heaven as a motivation to exercise discipleship today, yet that's exactly what Jesus seems to be pointing to. What He says is, "I'm looking forward to having them back with Me. But in the meantime, there's a job to do." In Philippians 1 Paul was gripped by the same challenge. "I want to depart and be with Christ which is far better, but there's work to do here. That's why I've been left on this planet, and I'd best be about it."

Without question, there's a sense in which all of us would rather be in heaven in the presence of the Lord with a perfect building already completed, enjoying its fruits. Yet there is much more to be done here before our eternity of enjoyment.

This past spring Back to the Bible moved into a beautiful new facility, a renovated building on the outskirts of Lincoln. It seemed like forever before the move could happen, and for our staff members who moved to the new building it was a time of great joy.

But the work my colleagues Woodrow Kroll, Allen Bean, our studio crew, and I perform is so closely associated with the studios—which were not yet complete in the new building—it was necessary for us to remain at what Dr. Kroll fondly refers to as "the mother ship." There we continue to record and produce radio programs and write messages for the ministries of Back to the Bible.

Sure, we'd rather be in the new building, and our colleagues would prefer to have us there. But right now it just isn't the time. In the same way, Jesus tells His Father, as His men listen, "I'd prefer to have these men with Me, beholding Our eternal glory. Right now, however, they need to remain as lights in the world, showing forth that glory, fulfilling the process of discipling."

## ENDNOTES

1. (Colorado Springs, Colo.: Focus on the Family Publishers, 1992).
2. Francis A. Schaeffer, "The Mark of the Christian," *Christianity Today* (March 6, 1995): 32–33.
3. Ibid., 33.
4. Dawson Trotman, "The Need of the Hour," *Discipleship Journal,* Vol. 11 (January 1991): 33.

## Chapter Twelve

---

# FINAL REVIEW

*I have declared to them Your name,*
*and will declare it . . . (John 17:26).*

In 1903 a single individual with 17 followers began an effort to take over the world. By 1918, that number had increased to 40,000, and with his followers, Vladimir Ilych Lenin secured control of the 165 million people in Russia.

In less than fifty years the Communist movement had gained control over a third of the world's population.

Many who have written and talked about discipleship have pointed to the Communists' commitment and perseverance in an attempt to motivate Christians to discipleship. Certainly, many in the Communist movement described themselves as fanatics, their lives dominated by that one overshadowing factor, the struggle for world domination by Communism. They focused on a cause to fight for and a clear-cut purpose in life. Like one young college student who converted to Communism in Mexico, many of them said, "There is one thing in which I am in dead earnest and that is the Communist cause. It is my life, my business, my religion, my hobby, my sweetheart. . . . I work at it in the daytime and dream of it at night. Its hold on me grows, not lessens, as time goes on. Therefore I cannot carry on a friendship, a love affair, or even a conversation without relating it to this force which both drives and guides my life."[1]

Certainly, many who followed the cause of Communism wound up putting Christ's disciples to shame with their commitment, zeal, and steadfastness. However, there's been an amazing development in recent years—the flaming torch of Communism has flickered and burned out.

First, there was Tianamen Square. Then the Iron Curtain parted. The Berlin Wall came down piece by piece. (I know, because my son, Brent, and I chipped out a few of the pieces to bring home to America!) Finally, there was the collapse of the Soviet Union.

Communism is no longer the major world force it once was. Almost everywhere, its dominance is being challenged and its iron fist is rusting away. Yet the cross of Jesus Christ and His mighty army of followers continues.

What's the difference? Clearly the success of discipleship cannot be determined by the level of commitment by the disciples. Even among Christians, discipleship was not meant to distinguish between different levels of commitment of believers. Every believer was intended to be a disciple, plugged into a vital growing relationship with the Savior, being mentored and in turn reaching out to mentor others in the faith.

However, Christian discipleship is unique because it provides both the path to life and the process of growth.

As Jesus concluded His intercessory prayer just moments before He was to cross the Kidron Brook and be arrested by soldiers led by one who had been numbered with His disciples, Jesus again addressed His Father with words of relationship and purpose for the men He had called and mentored.

## THE PATH OF LIFE

Earlier in His ministry, the disciples had heard Him say, "I am the way, the truth, and the life. No one comes to the Father except through Me" (John 14:6). Now, addressing His Father as the "righteous Father," Jesus contrasted the ignorance of the world at large of the Father with the fact that these His men had followed the one way to God. That Way was through the Savior who knew His Father intimately and who had made Him known to these men.

It's important to note that Jesus was not talking about

simply knowing facts but about a personal knowledge. Certain facts about God are available to the world, but most people have not acted on the revelation they have received and come to know the Father in a personal way.

From the beginning Jesus had been with the Father. John had used words we could translate "face to face with God" (1:2). No one knew the Father more intimately than the Son.

Jesus pointed out how, in contrast to the world, these men had come to know the Son whom the Father had sent. They were about to be indwelt and empowered by the Spirit, and they had come to experience authentic life. As Peter had confessed earlier, "Lord, to whom shall we go? You have the words of eternal life. Also we have come to believe and know that You are the Christ, the Son of the Living God" (6:68–69).

I have many friends who have come to personal faith because someone cared enough to disciple them. The process pointed them to the Savior who came from the Father and to the conviction that they needed to trust in Him as their only way to God.

Paul modeled this aspect of discipling with Timothy, whom he called "my true son in the faith." While his mother and grandmother had sowed the seeds of their faith in Timothy, it seems from the language of Scripture that Paul became the catalyst through whom Timothy placed his trust in the Lord Jesus.

Apparently the same thing happened with the core group of believers in Thessalonica. Paul had spent a brief period of time—identified by Luke as three Sabbath days—explaining the Gospel, and many had come to the faith. Paul recognized his relationship with these believers as resembling that of a nursing mother with a little child (1 Thess. 2:7–10). He sought to set a godly example for them, to protect them, and to nourish them with love. As they grew in the faith, his relationship shifted to become more like a father who seeks to equip his children to conduct themselves in a manner worthy of the family (1 Thess. 2:10–12). To do so, Paul encouraged, comforted, and urged them to live lives pleasing to the Lord.

Finally, as they grew up in the faith, he related to them more as brothers and sisters in Christ, focusing on his desire to see them continue living as mature Christians, serving together with him in the spread of the Gospel and bringing him ultimate joy in the Lord (v. 19).

In a sense Paul's relationship with Timothy and the Thessalonians was like that of Jesus with His men. He had declared to them the Father's name—representing everything the Father was—and He continued to declare it. They learned from Him, and through that knowledge they grew.

Yet there was much more than just content. As Juan Carlos Ortiz points out, "Discipleship is not a communication of knowledge or information, it is a communication of life. Discipleship is more than getting to know what the teacher knows, it is getting to be what He is."[2]

So it was with Jesus. He had not only declared to them His name. His motivation was to extend to them the love that existed in its purest form between the Father and the Son.

## The Process of Growth

This process of growth both included content and transcended content. It is as John Hatfield likes to describe it, "life on life." As John points out, "Teaching the Word and discipleship go hand in hand. It's impossible to do it apart from the Word, but it's certainly much more than just a curriculum or content. It's life touching life."

John Hatfield told me about Tracy. "He lived in our home for ten months, just moved out about six months ago. When he moved into our home, he watched everything we did. My wife, Kathy, had a major influence on him because he asked her all sorts of questions, to get a woman's perspective. He watched us raise our children, asked questions about that, how my wife and I relate to each other. You have to be an open book."

As I think about the individuals I've been privileged to disciple, I see strong evidences of both content and life-impact. The same thing has been true for those whose mentoring has left its indelible mark on me. It wasn't just the content of Alden Gannett's preaching, but the character of his life plus the content of his teaching. It was both the compassionate concern of Phil Hook and Charles Ryrie, and the challenging way they motivated me to interact with and apply the Scriptures.

And hopefully that same process has impacted the lives of Scott, Bill and Gary, Jim and Danny, Ken and Kent, Melvin and Billy, and others I've had the privilege to mentor in the faith.

## THE POWER OF SERVICE

There's one final thing. Jesus' discipling process ultimately prepared His men for the empowering legacy He left; as He described it, "I in them."

There are two aspects to these incredible three words. The first is the power of the indwelling Christ; the second, the permanent legacy it leaves.

In almost interchangeable fashion Jesus spoke of being *in* His disciples and the Spirit's being *in* them. The point is, we have God's person and power resident within to provide us with everything we need for life and godliness. We don't have to pull it off on our own, come up with a plan, or implement some strategy apart from Him. That's the great news about discipling. It's not something we have to do in and of ourselves. In the context of describing discipleship, the Lord assured His men of His presence within and the power He alone can provide.

Second, discipleship is the means by which we leave a lasting legacy in this world. At the beginning of this section I talked about cycles. I began to learn those principles of discipleship from those who initially mentored me when I was a young man at the outer edges of my teens. Last year I celebrated the tenth anniversary of my thirty-ninth birthday, and as the big "5–0" looms ever closer, I recognize that life is indeed like a vapor that appears for a short time, then vanishes.

In recent days, I've had the opportunity to try to communicate some of the things I hold dear to my son, Brent, who is now a sophomore in college. One of my most passionate desires is to so impact his life that he will come through the process and wind up leaving a lasting legacy for Christ himself. I feel the same kind of passion for those younger individuals in the faith I've had the privilege of mentoring in the past and those with whom I'm working in the present.

I think that's part of what Jesus had in mind in this last phrase of His prayer before His men when He said "I in them." I believe He was thinking beyond the disciples themselves to the church's continuing ministry of disciple-making as His lasting legacy on earth. After all, as He expressed earlier, He had glorified the Father by finishing the work He had been given to do. He was about to complete His ultimate work at the cross, but He had now finished the task expressed in the following statements.

- He had shown them what the Father was like, manifesting His name to them.
- He had given them the words that brought them to faith and eternal life.
- He had prayed for them, interceding for their protection, provision, and growth.
- He had protected them, shepherded them, and encouraged them through the difficulties of life and ministry.
- He had taught them the Word from His Father, the entire counsel of God, so they would have provision for sanctification and service.
- Now He was sending them forth into the world to repeat the process He had completed with them.

Yes, He was God, about to be crucified, resurrected, and ascended into heaven.

He would leave these men the legacy of His work of mentoring, the product of Master discipleship.

He would be in them as they carried on the work He had entrusted them to do through His power.

And for each of us who are growing as followers of the Master, the legacy lives on today.

### ENDNOTES

1. McDonald, *True Discipleship*, 34.
2. Ortiz, *Disciple*, 105.